In Praise of *Is God in That Bottle Cap*

"*Is God in That Bottle Cap* is a great book from a truth-seeker. It is both engaging and inspiring. I would love to see this book in the hands of practitioners of all paths for self-realization."

—**Vijayendra Pratap, Ph.D.**, Founder/Director of SKY Foundation, President of the Yoga Research Society, Author (*Beginning Yoga, Yoga Vision, Secrets of Hatha Vidya*)

"Finally a book about meditation that speaks to the 21st Century! Sambalino searches for "Truth," not with the usual loftiest of someone better than the rest of us—he explores and discovers so unapologetically, so enthusiastically, with the devoutness of a teenager who has just fallen in love and marries for life (which he also has done!). His lifelong practice is a breath of fresh air, a tale of encouragement that anyone can find the truth no matter where you go—and oh the places he goes!"

—**Katie Hyde**, Director/Producer, Founder of Indie City Films

"... readers should certainly enjoy this absorbing book. A lively and intensely readable story of one man's use of a variety of spiritual practices to reveal the nature of reality."

—*Kirkus Reviews*

"John Sambalino's life has had many "wake-up" moments, and he describes these engagingly. I got the sense that John brought forward into this life many talents from the past, and has deepened his relationship with Reality through his earnest commitment to practice and inquiry. A fun ride and informative read."

—**Jeff Cox**, retired president of Snow Lion Publications

"... a page-turning journey ... Sambalino is a gifted storyteller who compellingly shares his spiritual journey to inspire others. ... **Highly recommended** for fans of Ram Dass (*Be Here Now*) and Paramahansa Yogananda (*Autobiography of a Yogi*)."

—**Blueink Review**

"... an engaging combination of autobiography and philosophical treatise. ... Obviously composed to help others make their way to the truth, *Is God in That Bottle Cap?* presents the example of one man's striving, some of it seemingly haphazard, much of it sincerely aimed at an ultimate goal. By showing himself to be a regular guy gradually growing into this knowledge, Sambalino offers readers hope of success in their own personal journeys."

—**Self-Publishing Review** ★★★★

IS GOD IN
THAT BOTTLE CAP?

IS GOD IN THAT BOTTLE CAP?

A Search for Truth

John D. Sambalino

Vanishing
Circle Press

Vanishing
Circle Press

Email: vanishingcirclepress@gmail.com
www.isgodinthatbottlecap.com

Library of Congress Control Number: 2018912589

ISBN 978-1-7326578-0-9

Book cover design by www.jdandj.com

To my family, friends, and acquaintances, all of whom make life's journey so full and interesting.

Reality is merely an illusion, albeit a very persistent one.

—Albert Einstein

CONTENTS

ACKNOWLEDGMENTS

Having heard me speak about the benefits of meditation and the "reality" of life, many people over the years have said that I should write a book, and for over forty years I had been planning to do just that. For whatever reason, the time never seemed right and I kept putting it off. I need to thank my friend Gabriella Savelli for motivating me to sit down and just do it. Pulling out a stack of notebooks I had been filling up for decades, I started writing.

It's been a long undertaking, but I've enjoyed every minute of it and I want to thank my friend Rich Alleger, a retired executive with Rodale Press, for his expertise in guiding me through the whole process.

Lastly I want to thank my wife, Niki, for all her love and support. She is the rock that has enabled me to pursue my inner journey of self-discovery, while at the same time experiencing all the joy of a wondrous family life. I couldn't have done it without you.

INTRODUCTION

What's it all about? What's it really all about—reality, the universe, spirituality, God? These are questions I started asking myself at a very young age. I had this innate sense that the world that surrounds us couldn't possibly be as it appeared. There must be some hidden reality, something unseen that I could not perceive or understand. Was I really this person trapped in a small body, just waiting to grow old and die? It couldn't possibly be true. As a child, I had no idea where to turn to discover this hidden reality, this Ultimate Truth that I knew would somehow hold the answers I was seeking. The priests in the Catholic church, the religion in which I was raised, talked about God, heaven, and the afterlife, but their words seemed hollow. They didn't appear to have any firsthand knowledge of the tenets they were preaching. It was not until I entered college and read a book that spoke about enlightenment that I came to believe that there was a way to obtain what I had hopelessly yearned for—I would need to become enlightened. At first I thought intellectually acquired knowledge would lead me to enlightenment and the answers I sought. I then came to realize that the answers lay not on the outside, but on the inside. The reality was there; I just couldn't access it. I would need to travel inward to uncover what I was looking for. I have been meditating now for forty-four years. This is the story of my journey and what I have discovered.

Vedic *rishis*, or seers, would say that we are ignorant of our true nature. Christian mystics describe it as forgetfulness. Now, you may ask, what does ignorance or forgetfulness of our true nature have to do with discovering the Ultimate Truth? Everything! For everyone (and everything) is the Ultimate Truth. Now, you may say, "I am not this Ultimate Truth, this Ultimate Reality," and that is the problem, and the solution—the start and the end of our search. It is the answer to the ultimate question: Who am I?

So how do we move forward? What is it that we need to do? It is both the easiest and the hardest of all things, as all we have to do is remove the ignorance and remember. And yes, this is going to be much more involved than a simple question-and-answer session.

How can you get everything you want? How can you have answers to all of your questions? It's really quite simple—have no wants and no questions. Sounds like a cop-out, I know. The problem with this undertaking is that the medium we use is language—words—the medium of the mind and intellect, and this task goes far beyond the capabilities of both mind and intellect. So how do we proceed? As best we can. While I can't give you answers, hopefully I can present some interesting concepts and point you in a direction or two to help you on your way. That being said, this much I can assure you: At some point along your journey to explore what it's all about, two things will happen—questions and answers will start to merge and dissolve into a sense of knowing, and you will begin to realize that the *knowing* that everything dissolves into is you!

So what is this Ultimate Reality, this Ultimate Truth that we are looking for? Something is true if it is in accordance with fact or reality, or is accurate or exact. For this definition, truth is relative to time and place. If I look out my window and it's a beautiful sunny day out, this is a truth for this time and place. It's not always sunny and nice out, but for this time and place, it is. During one time and place it was considered a *truth* that the Earth was flat. Beliefs that people have about so many things, beliefs they consider based on truth are, in fact, in a constant state of flux and subject to change as their understandings of the underlying "truths" evolve.

So what is always true and not bound by limitations of time and space—what I call the immutable Ultimate Truth? Look around you. What do you see or perceive with any of your senses that has always been, and will always be, for all times and places, true? Anything? Nothing! There is nothing in this manifest universe that is the Ultimate Truth, as this universe came into existence many billions of years ago, and at some point it will cease to exist. Look in a mirror. Do you see the Ultimate Truth? Hardly. You see a person who is constantly changing—physically, mentally, and emotionally. For you to be the Ultimate Truth, you would have had to exist before this universe came into being and still be around after its dissolution. You would have to be changeless and beyond both time and space. Look in that mirror again. If you are certain that you are constantly changing and not the changeless, immutable Ultimate Truth, you may want to reconsider, for that image in the mirror is not you; that body being reflected in the mirror is not you; neither are its thoughts and emotions. Look around you one more time. Are you sure there is nothing that is the Ultimate Truth, as everything is in a constant state of change? If you are, you may once again want to reconsider, for as you will soon discover, things are definitely not as they appear. Confused? Good! Let's get started.

PART ONE
THE SEARCH

Search: To try to find or discover something by looking or otherwise seeking carefully and thoroughly.

CHAPTER 1

Growing Up

Growing up in the 1950s, I hated Fridays. It was the worst day of the week for me. I was a real meat-eater. I thought there was nothing better than a big, fat chunk of extra-rare beef, almost mooing and blood oozing out. My grandfather loved telling the story about the time he and my grandmother were driving across New York state from Buffalo to Sea Cliff, Long Island, to visit their daughter (my aunt) and her family. I was five or six years old, and my grandparents took me along for the trip. We stopped at a nice restaurant along the way for dinner. The place was like an old country inn, with wooden tables and booths, and wood-paneled walls. My grandfather told the waitress that his grandson would like the prime rib. The waitress looked at him very apologetically and stated that she was sorry, but they did not have any children's portions on the menu.

For the Sambalinos, food was a very important part of all family gatherings, and the ability to eat huge portions was revered. Everyone in the family had a healthy appetite, but there was one member who stood out in his ability to eat large quantities of food, and that person was me. My body seemed to require massive amounts of food. It wasn't that I was overeating, as I didn't have an ounce of fat on me; I just ate a lot. When our waitress said they did not have any children's portions, my grandfather took this as an insult and direct attack on the character of his grandson. My grandfather laid down his menu as he looked the waitress directly in the eyes and bellowed out: "A child's portion! My grandson does not want a *child's* portion! He wants the biggest cut of prime rib on the menu! EXTRA RARE!"

Within minutes, I was presented with a ginormous slab of roast beef, barely warm, just the way I liked it. It was a beautiful sight, and I immediately proceeded to eat the entire thing. Just as I was finishing up, the chef and kitchen staff walked over to our table. Our waitress had gone back to the kitchen and informed them that this tiny kid was eating every bit of that huge cut of roast beef, and they all wanted to see it.

In those days, the Catholic church forbade eating meat on Friday. My mother was very strict in enforcing this rule. She truly believed that eating meat on Friday was somehow a sin that would keep you from going to heaven. I wasn't too sure about all this, but it wasn't that much of a problem, as it was only one day a week and something I could deal with. But there was one Friday when this rule became a problem for me. My family and I (Mom, Dad, and little sister, Nancy) had gone to visit my dad's brother and his family for the weekend. I really hadn't given too much thought to dinner until I saw my uncle lighting a match under a pile of charcoal as he fired up the grill. He went inside and returned with a plate of huge porterhouse steaks. My father and his side of the family were not Catholic. My mother and her side of the family were. When my parents got married, my father had agreed to let my mother raise the kids Catholic, just as long as we were not sent to Catholic school. For everything else, my mother had complete discretion. So here I was, eight or nine years old, seated at the dinner table, and facing this monumental dilemma. Sitting in front of me on the serving plate were picture-perfect piles of porterhouse steaks. Perfectly cooked. Extra rare.

My father said to my mom: "Oh, go ahead, let him have some. It's only one time, and it is not a big deal." My mother was emphatic, stating that it was Friday and I could not eat meat. She was really adamant about this, and I was not allowed to have any. The fact that I couldn't enjoy those steaks, and had to sit there eating a piece of fish while watching my dad and my uncle's family eating them, really bothered me. It wasn't my mother that I blamed, but rather the church for telling people that somehow eating meat on Friday was a sin.

When I was twelve years old, my family (now with the addition of my baby sister, Janet) moved from Buffalo to Haddonfield, a town in South Jersey, about six miles from Philadelphia. My mother joined the local Catholic church, where we attended Mass on Sunday. Sitting in church on Sundays was another thing that bothered me— just sitting there, in boredom, looking around, waiting impatiently for the time to pass. It was like sitting in school at the very end of the day, waiting to be dismissed. At least in school you could look out the windows or stare at the clock and watch the seconds tick by. The windows in church were all stained glass, so we couldn't look out, and there was definitely no clock. If there had been a clock in church, I'm sure I wouldn't have been the only one staring at it.

Church made me feel inadequate. I was a very self-confident kid, and I had this sense that no one was better than me. It wasn't that I was any better than anyone else; just that they weren't any better than me. Other people were better at sports, better students, better at all kinds of stuff; just not better people. Sitting in church, I came to realize that there was someone who was much better than I was. Not someone who was better at certain things, but rather someone who was a flat-out better person. That person was Jesus Christ. I sat in church wondering how it was possible that I could be so inferior, so inadequate, compared to Jesus. Something just didn't seem right. Some mistake must have been made. I could not understand how I could have been born as this lowly human being with no possibility whatsoever of reaching the heights of a super being. I had this idle dream on many an occasion that one day I would just *morph* into Christ, walk over to my parents, and casually announce: "Mom, Dad—I want to tell you something—I am Jesus Christ!"

CHAPTER 2

Off to College

In August of 1968 I went off to North Carolina State University to study engineering. My dad was an electrical engineer, and I wanted to be an engineer also. I went to the bookstore to buy books for my first semester, and when I was done I continued to browse, checking out the huge selection of books. In the martial-arts section, I picked up a book on karate. It seemed very technical and explicit, with lots of pictures. For $7.50, I couldn't pass it up.

Growing up, I had always wanted to study martial arts. When I was in middle school, I had this great book on judo. It had it all: Everything from defending yourself against a savage attack dog, to taking out some maniac coming at you with a hatchet. My neighbor Barry and I used to practice our moves on each other, trying to break each other's arms or choke each other out. Some guy from Japan moved into town and opened an aikido studio. I didn't know too much about it, but one of my friends enrolled in a class. He told me they got to throw people around, swing sticks, and jab fake knives at one another. It sounded great and I really wanted to sign up, but my parents said no go. It cost more than my parents wanted to spend, and I didn't have the money.

The karate book sat in my dorm room for several days until I had a chance to start reading it. Under the history section, it stated that karate, as practiced in Japan, traced its origin to the ancient Chinese art of ch'uan-fa. Legend has it that an Indian Buddhist monk, Daruma Tai-shi (Bodhidharma), traveled from India to China to teach Buddhism. He settled at a monastery called Shaolin-szu to teach Buddhism to the Chinese monks there. Daruma's disciplines were so intense that the student monks passed out from sheer physical exhaustion. Daruma explained to his students that although the aim of Buddhism was salvation of the soul, the body and soul went hand in hand and that without the necessary physical stamina, it was not possible to attain enlightenment. He set up a system of exercise based on the I Chin Ching sutra. The discipline was martial in nature, and the Shaolin monks who studied under Daruma became some of the greatest fighters ever known.

One section in the karate book was about Mizu No Kokoro (a mind like water). It professed that a calm mind was like the surface of undisturbed water. Such a mind would enable one to know an opponent's movements and intentions, even before that opponent actually made any movement at all. Another section spoke of Tsuki No Kokoro (a mind like the moon), a concept wherein one's mind was like moonlight that shined equally on everything in its range, enabling one to be aware of opponents' movements, even opponents who were out of view.

These were new concepts to me. I don't believe I

had heard the term "enlightenment" before. It was not a word I had ever heard my parents use, or my friends, teachers, or priests at church. I definitely didn't know anything about having the ability to "see" things happening all around you, even without actually seeing them, or knowing of someone's physical intentions before even the slightest hint of movement. This was all intriguing, and I wanted to pursue it. My newfound interest in karate wasn't mainly for the sake of fighting, but rather for self-development or "enlightenment." I pored over this book, and started practicing the movements and exercises. Wanting to learn more about enlightenment and all that it encompassed, I started reading books on Zen Buddhism.

Zen was difficult for me to understand. The concepts seemed foreign and incomprehensible. Every once in a while in my readings I'd start to feel that I was beginning to understand a bit of what they were saying, and then I'd turn the page to some short story that made no sense whatsoever to me, such as:

> *A monk asked Nansen: "Is there a teaching no Master ever preached before?"*
> *Nansen said: "Yes there is."*
> *"What is it?" asked the monk.*
> *Nansen replied: "It is not mind, it is not Buddha, it is not things."*

Still, I enjoyed reading books on Zen, and I acquired a half-dozen by various authors. I also started reading books on yoga. These books also talked about enlightenment, as did the Zen books and the karate book. I got a copy of *Autobiography of a Yogi* by Paramahansa Yogananda, an enlightened Indian master who came to the United States in the 1920s to introduce yoga to Americans. This book was absolutely fascinating. Yogananda talked about yogis in India who possessed all kinds of unbelievable abilities—the ability to be in two places at the same time, to levitate, to do all kinds of crazy stuff. It wasn't so much the abilities of these yogis that attracted me, but rather their state of mind, their state of being, their so-called state of enlightenment. My fascination with enlightenment brought me back to the many times I had sat in church on Sunday mornings feeling so inferior to Jesus and the hopelessness of my miserable situation. Now my situation no longer seemed so hopeless, for, as I understood it, Jesus must have been an enlightened master, much like the ones I was reading about in my books. My thoughts were: *If they could do it, and he could do it, well then I can do it.* I didn't know how I was going to obtain this so-called enlightenment. To my knowledge, I had never met anyone who was enlightened or, for that matter, anyone who was even trying to reach enlightenment. All I knew was that this was what I wanted. I wasn't sure when I would start my journey, what path to take, or even how to find a path to get on, but that was okay; at eighteen years old, I had all the time in the world.

Even though I had never heard of these higher states of consciousness, or this state of enlightenment, until I picked up that book on karate, all through my childhood I had had a sense that things were not as they appeared.

As a young child of about five years old, I remember lying in bed one night, crying uncontrollably. My mother came in to see what was the matter, but I could not calm myself or stop crying. For no apparent reason, I had been totally overcome by a terrifying fear of death that went right to the core of my being. I was going to die, and there was nothing that I or anyone else could do to stop it. Sobbing, I told my mother that I did not want to die. She said, "What are you talking about? You are not going to die, you're just a little kid. You have a long life in front of you." Even though I did not know one person who had ever died, I knew it was just a matter of time. I knew I had only a limited amount of time on Earth, and the days were ticking by. Somehow I wanted to stop the passage of this deadly time bomb. Although my fear was not alleviated, my mother was able to console me, and I laid my head down on my pillow and eventually fell asleep. I never cried again about dying, but that acute awareness of my limited time on Earth has never left me.

My parents had a beach house at the Jersey Shore where we spent every summer. In the summer of 1969, I went with my sister Nancy to visit one of her friends. Her friend's father, Captain Eckols, had purchased an old coast guard station, and he was fixing it up and renting out rooms to lifeguards. Captain Eckols was retired from the navy and had spent many years studying palm reading. He professed to be an expert, and was going to read everyone's palms. My girlfriend at the time was also with us. Captain Eckols had never met my girlfriend or me, and didn't know anything about us. When he read my girlfriend's palms he said he had never seen a money line like hers, and that she was going to come into a huge sum of money. Captain

11

Eckols had no way of knowing that my girlfriend, in fact, came from an extremely wealthy family. You would never have known it from meeting her, as she was very down-to-earth and unpretentious. Captain Eckols read everyone's palms, and was finally going to read mine. He looked at one palm and then the other, going back and forth looking at my palms, turning my hands to examine the edges, and shaking his head, saying, "I don't know what this means."

I said, "What do you mean you don't know what this means?"

Again, shaking his head, he said, "I don't know what these lines in your palms mean." I pressed him as to why he could not read my palms, and finally he said, "I'd know what they would mean if it were five-hundred years ago, but I don't know what they mean now."

I asked, "What would it mean, if it was five-hundred years ago?"

He said, "If it was five-hundred years ago, I'd say that you were a monk." In the summer of 1969, I had not spoken to anyone about my interest in spirituality.

Several years later, I was looking through some stuff I had stored in my parents' attic in Haddonfield when I came across one of my high school notebooks. On the cover was something I had written in high school. It was a paraphrase of a quote from C.S. Lewis, which said: "If nothing in this world satisfies you, maybe you weren't meant for this world."

During my second year of college at North Carolina State University, I decided that I no longer wanted to be an engineer. My plan now was to move to India and live in a cave and meditate until I became enlightened. Besides the cost of the flight, I knew I wouldn't need much money once I got there. I also knew that when I eventually moved back to the US, it could be problematic if I had no money and no job. I thought it would be best to make some money first and put it away as a nest egg for my return. I didn't think I could earn the money fast enough as an engineer, so I decided that I would get a business degree and then go to law school. North Carolina State did not have a business program, so I decided to transfer to the University of South Carolina, where several of my friends were going to school. I finished up my second year at NC State, and in the fall of 1970 transferred to the University of South Carolina to finish my last two years, graduating in 1972 with a BS in Business Administration – Banking and Finance.

CHAPTER 3

Off to Law School

In March of 1973 I started my first year of law school at the University of Florida in Gainesville, Florida. Gainesville was a super fun place to go to school. It had a huge, 2000-acre campus with all kinds of stuff going on. There was always some major college sporting event happening, and the university presented numerous free concerts with top-name bands. What especially interested me were the events of a spiritual, New Age nature. While I continued to read books on yoga and Zen and anything else that I thought would help me on my way to enlightenment, I had a chance to meet some actual spiritual masters. One of the first people I remember seeing was Amrit Desai, the founder of the Kripalu Yoga Center in Sumneytown, Pennsylvania. Kripalu Yoga is a continuously flowing stream of yoga postures. Amrit's body would spontaneously flow through these postures while he was in a deep, meditative state. It was really quite impressive, and just watching him could bring you to a very relaxed, calm state of mind. But what really impressed me about Amrit was his state of mind. He was calm and relaxed and

14

seemed at ease in every situation. I remember the time he was giving a lecture in a hall at the University of Florida, taking questions from people in the audience, when some guy stood up to ask a question that was more of an inquisition. This guy was so nasty and full of hate that I wanted to crawl under my seat. I don't remember what the question was, but I'll never forget the questioner. His entire tone and manner toward Amrit was of outright hostility. I had no idea how Amrit could even respond to this guy, but without missing a beat, and with seemingly no effort on his part, Amrit answered him with love and kindness. There was the kind of love in his voice that you would expect to hear from a mother talking to her infant child. It was obvious that this guy's horrible, hateful question, which was actually a direct attack on Amrit, had no effect on him. He answered from a calm, relaxed, loving center that he always appeared to be in. This was something I wanted to achieve, and I believed it would come with spiritual development and understanding.

During my years of law school at the University of Florida (three years of law school and one year of tax school), I tried to see every spiritual master who came through town. I went to Mickey Singer's house on several occasions to see various spiritual masters. Mickey had a retreat center that was known as the Temple of the Universe. It wasn't much more than a small, secluded wooden house, on a few acres just outside of Gainesville. He had yogis, monks, and spiritual leaders of all kinds come to his place, which he opened to the public. One time he had this Zen monk at his house talking about Zen and his life in general. The guy was interesting enough, but somehow he seemed a little off to me. We were all outside during a break, and I saw him light a cigarette. I went over to this Zen monk and asked him, "What's going on with the smoking?" I couldn't understand how someone who was supposedly enlightened, or close to it, could have the desire to do something so detrimental to their health as smoke a cigarette. He gave me some story about his higher state of consciousness and how smoking really didn't affect him. Well maybe it was my defect, but this was not what I wanted to see or hear from a monk, so I grabbed my stuff and left.

Another time in Gainesville, I went to a talk that was presented by followers of a guru who called himself the "Perfect Master." I was in my early twenties, and this guy was in his mid-teens. I remember hearing stories of him taking water cannons and hosing down his followers. He wasn't at this event, only some of his followers who played an audiotape about their organization. I didn't know who was speaking on the tape, but to me the person talking seemed totally out of it, almost delusional. When the tape was over I learned that the person on the tape was this teenage "Perfect Master." Needless to say, I couldn't get out of that place fast enough.

CHAPTER 4

Down to the Keys

During my eight years of college, law school, and tax school, I spent every spring break in Key West and the Florida Keys. A group of my friends and I would go down for a week or so and camp out at Bow Channel Campground, twenty miles from Key West. The spring of 1974 was no exception, and after completing my first year of law school, I packed up my VW van, threw my 650 Triumph Bonneville motorcycle in the back, and headed down to the Keys with my best pal, Rocky.

Rocky was my dog whom I had gotten three-and-a-half years before, when I was a junior at the University of South Carolina. Rocky was the best dog ever—super smart, obedient, and tough as nails. I could write a whole book on Rocky; the stories are endless. I actually got Rocky through a trade-in on a dead dog. My roommate Joe and I had bought a puppy at the local pound in Columbia, South Carolina. The dog appeared to be fine, but after a couple of days, he died in his sleep. The next morning, we put him in a paper bag, took him back to the pound, and asked for another dog. The attendant said, "No problem," and let out about a dozen little puppies to run around the room, so that we could pick one. This guy also had his own dog in the room, an adult German shepherd who appeared to weigh about 80 or 90 pounds. All the puppies were cute, and all but one started jumping around and playing with each other. A fuzzy black puppy that could fit in the palm of your hand ran straight over to the German shepherd and tried to kill him. He jumped up, trying to latch onto the much-larger dog's neck, but there was no way he could reach it, so he had to settle on biting him on his lower legs and knees. The German shepherd just looked at him as if to say, "You have got to be kidding." We picked up the little black dog and told the guy at the pound that this was the one we wanted.

That first night, we put Rocky in the kitchen and placed a fireplace screen across the doorway so he couldn't get out. We went back to the bedroom, and about two seconds later Rocky came strolling in. I picked him up and took him back to the kitchen. The screen was still across the doorway, and I had no idea how he got out. I placed him on the floor in the kitchen, on the other side of the screen, and stepped back to watch. The fireplace screen was about thirty inches high and had very small mesh. Rocky walked over to the screen and stood up on his hind legs with his front paws leaning up against it. Now, Rocky was little, only weighing two-and-a-quarter pounds, and stretched out he couldn't have been much longer than eight inches. He put his tiny little claws into the screen's mesh, climbed to the top, dropped over, and walked over to me, wagging his tail. That night he slept in my room, as he did every night. The next day, he started his commando training.

Now, if you're a PETA member, please don't be alarmed. I loved Rocky and I never hurt him in any way, but his training was intense and complete. First up was coming when I called him. No matter what he was doing, I wanted Rocky to come immediately when I called him. I put him in the backyard and got out an old fishing pole and attached the line to his collar. Every time I called him, I would immediately reel him in. He got the message: When I called, he came. Next came sitting training. I used to do a lot of pull-ups, and I had a pull-up bar across the top of my bedroom doorway. I put Rocky on a box under my pull-up bar and put a rope over the bar with one end tied around his neck, and the other end in my hand, and told him to sit. Sit he did, and he didn't move a muscle. There was no way Rocky could have hurt himself, as if he fell off or jumped off the box, I would have let go of the rope. He didn't know this and would just sit there, as still as a statue. After a little bit I would take the rope off his neck and let him off the box, hugging him and telling him what a good boy he was.

I also trained Rocky to not be afraid of being put into any kind of container, no matter how small. I'd put him into small boxes, where he would just barely fit, and close him up. After a few moments, I would let him out and again tell him what a good boy he was. Rocky also went through height training. When he was little, I'd put him on a chair and have him jump off it. As he grew, I'd increase the height, having him jump off tables and eventually off the top of the refrigerator. Rocky also received swimming training from our roommate Jimmy, who was the captain of the swimming team at the University of South Carolina. When Rocky was tiny, we'd be out in the woods walking on logs across streams, and Jimmy would gently bump him from behind with his foot, pushing him off and into the water when he least expected it. Rocky would sink under and then pop up and swim to shore. When Rocky was older, I'd take him out into the ocean with me. He loved fetching, and I'd go out into chest-deep water with him and wave a stick over my head, and then hold the stick under the water as far down as I could reach and tell him to get the stick. Rocky would go under the water and swim down, and get the stick from my hand and bring it to the surface.

Rocky also received other training, including attack training, ladder climbing, and childproofing, so he would never growl or bite a child, no matter what they did to him. Now, you might think I'm a little crazy, and I wouldn't necessarily disagree, but there was a method to my madness.

A few examples: I used to fly a lot, and Rocky had his own flying crate and went with me. Airport security was very different back then. I would take Rocky and his crate outside to baggage, where we would meet the baggage handlers. The baggage handlers would say, "Let's put Rocky (who now weighed about 45 pounds) into his crate and then lift him onto the baggage cart."

I'd say, "No, let's just put the crate on first."

And they'd say, "Put him in first," as it would be easier.

I'd say, "Trust me." We'd put the empty crate onto the baggage cart, and I would then open the door and tell Rocky to get in. Rocky would dive up into the open crate and I'd shut the door. The baggage handlers would go crazy, asking if he was a circus dog and where I got him. (Over the years, a number of people asked me where I got this dog and wanted to know if I would sell him. He really was unbelievable.)

One time during spring break, we stopped to visit some friends who were staying on the third floor of a hotel in Ft. Lauderdale. The hotel did not allow dogs, so I went out to my van and emptied a suitcase and told Rocky to get in. He got in, barely fitting, and I closed the suitcase up and carried him in past the front desk, into the elevator, and up to the third floor. When we got to the room, I opened the suitcase and he popped out, wagging his tail just as proud as he could be.

One time we were down at the shore in New Jersey and Rocky got out. I called for him and he came running down the street toward me as fast as he could. Just as he was about to dash across the street to reach me, a car flew toward him. I just yelled, "Rocky, sit!" He came to a streaking halt, almost sliding to a sitting position. The car passed by and I said, "Come on," and Rocky jogged safely across the street.

Once, Niki and I (more about her later) were floating on an inner tube in a quarry. Rocky was up on the ledge of the quarry, about ten or twelve feet above the water. He was barking to come to us, so I just called him. He exploded off the side and into the water below.

Another time, Niki was home alone in my house in Gainesville on Halloween when three men walked into the house. Rocky saw them coming and chased them out of the house, biting one and moving on to another who tried to climb a tree. Niki called him off, and Rocky walked back into the house. I have hundreds of stories, but you get the picture—Rocky was one of a kind.

During this particular spring break, we met up in the Keys with a bunch of friends with whom I had gone to the University of South Carolina. We spent our days at Bow Channel, hanging out, exploring, snorkeling, and looking for lobsters. At night we drove into Key West to watch the sunset and hit the bars. My friends had driven down to the Keys in a huge rented Winnebago. One night, about a dozen of us piled in and headed into Key West. We parked on Duval Street, about a block from our destination, Lou's Bar. I was the last person to get out of the Winnebago, and as I got out and turned to walk toward Lou's, I spotted three girls sitting on the curb. I ran over to see if I could get them to go to Lou's with us. One of the girls was an absolute knockout. I mean a real beauty. They said they would like to go into Lou's with us, but they were only nineteen years old. I had just turned twenty-four. I said, "No problem. Come with me."

Lou's had huge open-air windows all across the front that were waist-high from the inside and chest-high from the outside. I told the girls to walk down the sidewalk to the last window and wait there. I then went in the front door, got carded, grabbed my friends, and walked over to a large vacant table next to the same window. I told the girls to get ready, then all my friends jumped up at the table, causing a friendly ruckus that blocked the window from view. A couple of us grabbed the girls' arms and pulled them in. All three girls were attractive, but it was the beauty, Niki, whom I could not take my eyes off of. The girls turned out to be freshmen at the University of Florida, the same university where I was going to law school. When we left Lou's, we told the girls to come visit us at Bow Channel Campground, and the next day all three showed up. Niki didn't seem as interested in me as I was in her, but she didn't have a chance against my secret weapon—Rocky. Rocky never had to be on a leash because he just hung out with me. She had no idea whose dog he was, or even if he belonged to anyone. When she found out that he was my dog, I think that kind of sealed it. We spent the rest of spring break together and instead of going our separate ways, we both went back to Gainesville. What would have been just a spring-break fling turned out to be a long-term romantic relationship—a *very* long-term romantic relationship. Niki and I dated for eight years. This year we celebrated our 36th wedding anniversary.

CHAPTER 5

Learning to Meditate

We got back to Gainesville, and I started my second year of law school. Niki and I were together all the time. I told her of my plans to move to India and live in a cave and meditate until I became enlightened. She told some of her friends what my plans were, and her friend Ilene came over to the house to talk to me. It turns out Ilene had been doing Transcendental Meditation (TM) for a couple of years. She said, "Why don't you learn TM and start meditating now? That way, when you move to India you'll already have a few years of meditation under your belt, and you'll be that much further along." It made perfect sense to me.

Gainesville had its own TM center, so I called them, plopped down my $35, and learned to meditate. Transcendental Meditation is a mantra meditation that was spread throughout the world by Maharishi Mahesh Yogi. You are given a mantra, a Sanskrit word (sound) that you effortlessly and silently repeat to yourself. When done properly, the mind relaxes and settles down, and thoughts go to their subtlest level and then drop away altogether as

you transcend into the transcendence; that silent awareness beyond thought from where everything originates,
including thoughts.

My first meditation was beyond fantastic. As my
mind settled, my consciousness, or awareness, began to
expand and then become unbounded. This was accompanied by some really strange body sensations. My extrem-
ities swelled and expanded. One of my arms felt like it
had disappeared or fallen off. The sense of well-being was
overwhelming. After twenty minutes I was instructed to
stop meditating and open my eyes. I sat in this super-re-
laxed state of contentment. While the experience had been
over-the-top wonderful, surprisingly it was not a new one
for me. I had had these same sensations many times as a
child, the last of which I could remember having when I
was ten or eleven years old. I had totally forgotten about
them, and it wasn't until they were re-experienced during
my first meditation that the memories returned. As a
child, I didn't remember giving much thought to these
sensations, which I now knew were something that could
accompany transcending. They would just come for no apparent reason, last for a few moments to several minutes,
and then go just as quickly and uneventfully as they had
arrived. Many times these sensations would come just as I
was beginning to fall asleep. Not knowing what they were
or when they might come, these experiences, though very
enjoyable, didn't seem to register in my psyche, and once
gone, I don't remember ever giving them a second thought.

The crazy experiences I had during my first meditation did not frighten me in any way, as I had had strange,
out-of-body sensations before, not only during my child-

hood experiences of transcending, but also in my later years of experimenting with drugs.

I smoked marijuana for the first time in the summer of 1968, just after graduating from high school. Though I found it enjoyable, I only smoked marijuana occasionally until the start of my junior year of college at the University of South Carolina in the fall of 1970, when I started smoking pot daily. Over the next few years I also experimented with psilocybin mushrooms and peyote cactus. Psilocybin mushrooms and peyote cactus contain psychedelic compounds that can cause vivid visuals, distort the sense of reality, and alter time perception. Psilocybin and peyote, both native to North America, have been used since prehistoric times by many cultures in their religious rites and ceremonies. Though having some similarities, my experiences during my meditation had a totally different quality than those induced by drugs. Psychedelic drug use, though pleasant, caused a sense of confusion and disorientation. During meditation, my mind had a heightened sense of stillness and awareness, and everything that occurred seemed very natural. The sense of peace and well-being was overwhelming.

Returning home, I couldn't wait to meditate again. The instructions I received when I learned TM were to meditate for twenty minutes, twice a day, once in the morning before breakfast, and again before dinner. I was so excited to repeat the experiences of my first meditation. The problem was, my next meditation, while enjoyable, was nowhere near as great as my first. Even so, I looked forward to my next meditation after that. This went on for months. I looked forward to meditating, but the meditations weren't that great. For many of them, it was like nothing was happening at all. I sat quietly, silently repeating my mantra, but it took a long time for my thoughts to settle, if they settled at all. I was so anxious to have a great meditation, and nothing was happening. Most of my meditations were shallow, and it felt like I was basically just sitting there with my eyes closed. I started to skip meditations, doing only one each day. Then I began missing whole days. Getting no positive reinforcement, meditation started to become a chore. Even though I knew it was good for me, it became something I had to make myself do.

I kept up with my readings on books about spirituality, and my sporadic meditating, hoping for something to happen. Nothing did. After several months, I came to an intellectual understanding that has grown exponentially over the years and is something I will describe in-depth later. Meditation has to be effortless, and whatever happens is what is supposed to happen. The mind does not take itself to the transcendental state, and no amount of effort will take it there. The mind merely settles during meditation, and from that settled state our awareness drops effortlessly into transcendence. Effort on the part of the meditator keeps the mind from settling down. Trying to meditate and trying to have an experience will have the opposite effect. You just let go, effortlessly do the technique, and whatever happens, happens. On my next meditation I gave up trying and sat with no expectation of any specific result. My mind settled deeply, and I had a great meditation. The excitement returned and I couldn't wait to meditate again. I gave up all my efforts and I didn't care what happened during meditation. How did it work out?

All my meditations are great, and I always look forward to them. In fact, I haven't missed a day of meditating in over forty years.

CHAPTER 6

Learning Martial Arts

I never lost that early interest I had in martial arts. The University of Florida had a judo club, and I signed up as soon as I entered law school. Judo came very naturally to me, almost as if I had somehow done it before. I'm not talking about the elementary stuff that my neighbor, Barry, and I did as kids. I'm talking about some very high-level stuff, stuff that I had no way of knowing. I didn't have to think about what I was going to do on the mat; my body knew it instinctively.

As new students, we were all given white belts and taught some basic throws. After several weeks of training, the white belts were paired up with the next-level green belts to do randori, a one-on-one freestyle format where we tried to throw our opponents. The first two people went out on the mat for five minutes and tried to throw each other. The green belt may have thrown the white belt one time. The white belt could not throw the green belt. This went on for several five-minute matches. The green belts were able to throw the white belts maybe one or two times at most, but the white belts could not throw the green belts.

None of the throws that the green belts made seemed that great, and it mostly looked like a lot pushing and shoving. Then it was my turn.

I knew inherently that using force against force was not the way to throw someone. I wanted to get my opponent moving and off-balance, and then use his off-balanced movement to throw him. Most importantly, I wanted to get my opponent moving and off-balance before he knew what was happening. I understood that if you push on someone, his natural reaction is to push back with the same force and speed as your push. You push harder; he pushes back harder. You push more gently; he pushes back more gently. Even if I pushed ever-so-slightly, almost imperceptibly, I knew my opponent would naturally and unknowingly push back on me.

Facing each other in the center of the mat, my green belt opponent and I grabbed each other's gis, those thick white jackets that judo players wear. I quickly and forcefully pulled him toward me, and he immediately pulled back, but as he instinctively pulled me forward, I stepped forward, placing one of my legs behind him, and pushed him in the same direction that he was going—backwards; throwing him right onto the mat. Once he responded to my initial pull, I used a force, timing, and speed that never let him get back on balance, for as soon as he pulled away from my initial pull on him, I relaxed totally and moved forward, giving him nothing to pull on, and since there was nothing for him to pull on, he put himself immediately off-balance.

My partner got up and we grabbed each other's gis again, each holding one of the other's lapels and one of the other's sleeves. This time, instead of pulling my opponent forward, I pushed him straight back. He immediately pushed back on me, and as he did, I swung my left leg back and around and planted it firmly on the mat, while at the same time pulling him forward, accelerating his movement. He could not regain his balance, and I pulled him right over my right leg as he flipped onto the mat. This went on for the entire five-minute period of our randori. My partner never came close to throwing me, and I could throw him at will. I must have thrown him twenty times. Foot sweeps, hip throws, throws over my shoulder—everything worked. I wasn't sure exactly how I did what I did, as none of my throws were planned; I just did what came to me in the moment. I just responded to what was organically taking place.

A few weeks later, I did randori with another one of the more senior green belts. As we faced off, I grabbed this guy and pulled him hard and quick in a circular motion to my right. As he pushed back, I immediately changed directions and pulled him hard and fast in a circular motion to my left. As I did this, I picked up my right leg and, keeping it straight, swung it up and over as hard and as fast as I could, hitting him directly in his midsection. He cartwheeled over my extended leg, landing on his back. One of the brown belts immediately ran over to me. He wanted to know where I had learned that move. I told him I hadn't learned it; it just seemed to happen on its own in the moment. He told me that that throw was from a 5th- or 6th-degree judo black belt kata (exercise) that was used in training to show skill and technique, but he had never seen, or even heard of, anyone ever trying it in freestyle fighting, much less pulling it off and executing it. I told him I didn't know what to say—I wasn't thinking; it just happened.

A couple of months later, I was promoted to green belt. As part of the ceremony, I had to let everyone in our judo club throw me. I couldn't resist; I just had to stand there and let everyone throw me using whatever throw they wanted. We learned two important things in judo that we practiced in every class. The first was how to take a fall without getting hurt. The second was how to throw an opponent without injuring them.

We had learned a variety of falling techniques. One of my favorites involved a forward dive with one arm extended. As I hit the mat, I tucked my head and rounded my outstretched arm, rolling forward on the edge of my hand and arm, across my back, and coming to a standing position.

We had also learned techniques for safe throwing. Most judo throws are made with one hand holding onto one of the sleeves of your opponent's gi and the other hand holding onto their opposite lapel. On many of these throws, as you are throwing your opponent, you let go of their lapel and grab the same sleeve as your other hand, and just before they hit the ground you pull up on their sleeve with both of your arms to help them land safely on their back instead of on their shoulder. After being thrown by fifteen or twenty of my classmates, from white belts to black belts, a less experienced classmate didn't let go or pull up, and my shoulder hit the mat first. The pain was immediate.

Someone had to help me remove my gi, as I couldn't

take it off by myself. They then helped me get my T-shirt on. At the infirmary, they told me that I had separated my shoulder. It was going to take a month or two for it to heal, and I needed to keep my arm in a sling for a few weeks and rest the area.

Even though I couldn't participate, I went back to judo the next day. I wanted to see if I could pick up the moves by just watching. After a month of watching, I got back on the mat. I could walk through the moves with a partner, but I could not throw anyone, and no one was allowed to throw me, as my shoulder was still not healed and it hurt if I exerted my arm even slightly.

My partner during one of my limited practice sessions was a 2nd-degree black belt. I told him that he could not throw me as my shoulder was messed up, and he complained to Sensei (the head teacher) that he did not want to work with someone whom he could not throw. Sensei confirmed my injury to him and told him to go easy and just go through the moves, but no throwing. A few weeks later, my shoulder started feeling much better, about 90 percent, and I felt that I could now do randori. One of my first opponents was the 2nd-degree black belt who had been complaining a few weeks earlier that he was not allowed to throw me. Now he had his chance.

Even though my shoulder was not 100 percent and this guy outweighed me by fifteen or twenty pounds, I felt pretty confident that I could throw him. I was a little surprised when our match ended and I hadn't been able to, but not as surprised as he was. He was quite taken aback that he was unable to throw me, a newly promoted green belt. When we had done our practice session a few weeks earlier, my shoulder was so tender that I couldn't exert even the slighted amount of force against him. Now I was able to defend myself against every throw he tried.

The following month I got to do randori with Sensei. Our sensei was a math professor from Germany. He was a 3rd- or 4th-degree black belt, and about my size. He was also the former European judo champion for his weight class. When he took his position at the University of Florida, he had started the judo club. My shoulder was now completely healed and I could go full-on. I took him right to the ground. Everyone was a little surprised that I was able to throw Sensei. At our next class, one of my friends who was up for his black belt test came over to me. He said, "I heard you threw Sensei."

I said, "Yeah, I was able to get a throw in on him."

He said, "Congratulations, you're the first." Since starting the University of Florida Judo Club, no one had ever been able to throw Sensei. No brown belts, no black belts, and definitely no green belts.

I did judo for a year and enjoyed every second of it, but I decided that I wanted something a little more martial, so I moved on to karate, joining the Cuong Nhu Karate Club, founded by Sensei Ngo Dong, a professor of entomology who brought his style of karate with him from his native Vietnam. Master Dong had studied many forms of martial arts, including Vovinam (a Vietnamese system of self-defense), Wing Chun, Aikido, Shotokan Karate, Jujitsu, and Judo. He combined them into his system, which he named Cuong Nhu (hard soft). I did Cuong Nhu Karate for a couple of years and, like with judo, I liked it a lot. I wanted to continue studying martial arts as I moved along my spiritual path, but as I progressed I wanted something a little more internal, something that would be more complementary to my journey of self-discovery.

In the spring of 1977, I saw a flyer for a T'ai Chi Ch'uan class that was going to be starting up in Gainesville. I went to the introductory talk and discovered that T'ai Chi was exactly what I was looking for. T'ai Chi was founded between the twelfth and thirteenth centuries during the Sung Dynasty by Chinese boxer Chang San-Feng. Chang was a Taoist who studied at the Shaolin temple in his youth. Taoism, the original naturalistic philosophy of China, was based on the writing of Lao-tzu, advocating humility and religious piety, with emphasis on inner contemplation and mystical union with nature. While practicing mystical Taoist meditation, Chang perceived the form of a snake in combat with a bird. He saw that rather than meeting head-on and using force to fight force, the snake and bird coordinated with each other, trying to avoid direct opposition in order to penetrate each other's defenses. Chang deemed this principle of yielding and following as more in accord with Taoist principles than the hard and aggressive styles of the Shaolin monks, and he refined the Shaolin movements to develop a style known as nei chia, or inner school, which became the foundation of present-day T'ai Chi Ch'uan. The Yang Short Form style of T'ai Chi that was being offered in Gainesville was brought to the United States by the late Cheng Man-ch'ing, and the class was being taught by one of his senior students, Patrick Watson.

I signed up for the beginner class, which was taught for one hour a day for ten straight days. I immediately fell in love with T'ai Chi and found it to be a perfect complement to my meditation and spiritual pursuits. If yoga could be described as being flexible and stretchy like a rubber band, T'ai Chi was more like being soft like a ball of cotton, with an emphasis on total relaxation. Through effortless breathing, rhythmic movement, weight equilibrium, and focus on total relaxation, one develops chi, an energy that flows through the universe. The goal is not to move the body by physical effort, but rather to have the mind direct the chi, and have the chi move the body *at the direction of the mind.* Each night after class I would go to the gymnasium to practice the moves on my own for two more hours in front of a wall of full-length mirrors. I continued to practice T'ai Chi every day after the ten-day class ended, and over the next two years I attended every T'ai Chi class that was being offered in Gainesville. After that, I decided to become a T'ai Chi teacher, taking four weeks of T'ai Chi teacher training classes every year for the next ten years, studying two weeks at the school's main headquarters in New York City each winter and two weeks each summer at various college campuses in New England. While I no longer teach T'ai Chi, I do practice every day.

One instruction that is given to newcomers of meditation or martial arts is to not mix disciplines. You want to keep the purity of the teachings, and mixing them, especially by new students, only causes confusion. If you want to learn more than one martial art, it is usually better to start with only one and then, after a few years of practice, add another. With meditation practice, it is even more imperative for beginners to keep the teachings pure and not add your own changes or incorporate techniques from other practices. You want to pick a meditation practice and then stick with it and not jump from technique to technique or combine techniques.

When I started studying T'ai Chi, I had already been doing TM for two and a half years. Transcendental Meditation is a mantra meditation that uses a mantra to settle the mind and facilitate a transcendental experience. The mind and the body are connected, and as the mind settles down during TM practice, the body also relaxes and settles down. T'ai Chi can be considered a moving meditation in that by relaxing the body totally and moving through the form (a set of specific movements) in a slow, smooth, rhythmic fashion, a transcendental experience can be brought about. And again, as the mind and body are connected, as the body relaxes and settles during T'ai Chi practice, the mind also relaxes and settles. My thought was: *Can I somehow incorporate the body relaxation of my T'ai Chi practice into my TM practice without corrupting the integrity of the meditation in any way?* I believed that I could. As I sat for meditation with eyes closed, but before actually starting to meditate, I relaxed my body totally, letting go of everything. Then, keeping my body totally relaxed, I introduced the mantra. The result? I immediately transcended, dropping into that empty space almost instantaneously. Being able to let go of both body tension and mental effort really brought the depth of my meditations to a new level.

CHAPTER 7

Amrit Desai

In 1975 and 1976 I went on several retreats held at Amrit Desai's Kripalu Yoga centers in Summit Station and Sumneytown, Pennsylvania. During one summer visit, Amrit chanted and played his harmonium at the front of the room. I sat, eyes closed, in a meditative state, but my attention was drawn to the flies let in through the open windows that kept landing on my face and crawling across my cheeks and nose. Suddenly, in an instant, my awareness or consciousness "dropped." It was as if the floor had disappeared and I fell into another dimension. I was no longer my body or thoughts, but rather this "I" that was something totally separate and distinct. I still had a slight awareness of the flies that were crawling across my face, but they did not disturb me in the least, because the flies, my face, and all thoughts and sensations, were now 1,000 miles from this new, separate "I." It was a very overwhelming, yet blissful experience that lasted for only a brief minute. Then I returned to my normal state of consciousness, flies included.

In the summer of 1977, Amrit Desai's guru (spiritual teacher), Swami Kripalvananda, came from India to the United States for a visit. Amrit held a retreat at his Sumneytown center with Swami Kripalvananda, or Bapuji as he was known. I don't remember too much about the retreat, except for how much love Amrit had for his teacher. Bapuji told a story about an ancient guru and the extreme devotion his disciple had for him. Amrit was translating, and in the middle of the story he broke down in tears. It was a very emotional moment and everyone in attendance started to cry. But what I really remember about the retreat was the ride home. Shortly after leaving the ashram, my friends and I stopped to get gas. As the driver got out to pump the gas, everything just "stopped." My consciousness came to a standstill. The "I" that I had always known—my body, mind, and thoughts—was still sitting in the car, seeing and aware of all that was going on. But now there was another "I"—an "I" that was unquestionably the real me—and this "I" just sat there, silently aware of everything that was going on. This new "I," this consciousness, expanded outward in all directions, and seemed to be the medium in which everything was happening. It was separate from everything, yet everything and everyone, including me, was somehow an undivided part of it. This new "I" did not take part in anything, did not care what was happening, did not think anything about what was going on. It was just "there," silent and without movement, aware of everything. I knew immediately what was happening. I was having an experience of "witnessing," something that I had read about in my many books on yoga. This experience was somewhat similar to my experiences of transcending during meditation, except now I was not meditating. I was just sitting in the back of a car, eyes open and totally awake. This "I," which seemed to be my innermost consciousness, my real Self, was motionless, without thoughts, aware of everything. Aware of the gas station and everything and everyone around: The driver pumping the gas; the other cars and drivers at the gas station; myself, and the other people in our car; our driver getting back into the car and driving away; the scenery passing by as we drove down the road—everything. And again, there was no separation between this witnessing awareness and everything that was going on, for in some inexplicable way everything and everyone was a part of, and inside of, this newfound awareness. With this experience, which lasted maybe an hour, came a sense of peace, contentment, and joy.

CHAPTER 8

Learning the Siddhis

In 1977 word came out that Maharishi Mahesh Yogi, the founder of Transcendental Meditation, was offering a new program of advanced techniques to meditators—the TM-Sidhi Program. These advanced techniques, based on Patanjali's yoga sutras, or aphorisms, were known as far back as 3,000 BC and were codified by the Indian sage *Patanjali* sometime between 400 BC and 200 AD. Practicing these sutras would purportedly deepen one's meditative experiences and hasten the journey to enlightenment. Practicing these sutras would also supposedly endow the practitioner with certain supernormal abilities, or powers (siddhis, spelled "sidhis" by the TM organization), and included such things as super strength, the ability to heal oneself from illness, the ability to know everything (including objects obstructed from view or placed at a great distance), and the ability to levitate. I had read about these abilities and many more, in Paramahansa Yogananda's *Autobiography of a Yogi*. The course was going to be a sixteen-week, in-residence, intensive meditation course. You could not take the course if you smoked cigarettes (I did

41

not), and you could not drink alcohol or do recreational drugs (I did). I signed up for the course and immediately stopped drinking and getting high.

I had been smoking pot daily for the past seven years and drinking since I was fourteen. I had never considered myself a drug addict or someone who had a drinking problem; I just enjoyed drinking and getting high. During the preceding seven years, I had graduated from the University of South Carolina with a Bachelor of Science in Business Administration – Banking and Finance (receiving the Dean's Certificate of Outstanding Academic Achievement), and graduated from the University of Florida College of Law, receiving both my Juris Doctor (having made both the Dean's Honor List and High Honor List), and my Master of Laws in Taxation. While earning my Master of Laws, I also taught Legal Writing and did Supervised Teaching in Federal Income Taxation at the University of Florida College of Law. During that entire seven-year period, I never went to class high, and I never did any drugs or drank until after I had done all my homework. That being said, my plan was always to one day stop doing all drugs completely and just meditate. I did not plan on stopping all future drug use now; just drug use for the duration of the course. I never planned to stop drinking.

The siddhi course was broken into two parts: An eight-week preparatory section to be taught at various locations throughout the country; and the actual siddhis, which were to be taught during a second, eight-week section at the TM retreat center in Livingston Manor, New York. Siddhis are mental techniques that one does as part of an overall, extended meditation practice. They are done, or introduced, from the transcendental state of consciousness that is experienced during meditation. The more established one is in the transcendental state, the more powerful and effective the siddhis are. Maharishi wanted to be sure that people were in a deep transcendental state when learning and practicing the siddhis, thus the eight-week preparatory course.

I took my siddhi prep course in Florida, starting in November of 1977. The first things we learned on the course were postures, or asanas, of hatha yoga. Practicing the postures of hatha yoga opens the many channels, or nadis, in the body through which prana flows, thus allowing the prana to flow more freely and properly throughout the body. Prana is a subtle life force, or energy, that exists everywhere and flows through everything in the universe. Prana flowing strongly and properly through the body can help liberate the mind (making it calm, peaceful, and content) and expand consciousness. It also helps keep the body strong, healthy, and energetic. In Chinese meditation, martial arts, and traditional medicine, prana is called qi (chi) and the nadis are known as meridians. In Japan, as in China, the nadis are known as meridians, but prana is called ki. Also taught on the prep course were pranayamas, or yogic breathing exercises. As with hatha yoga, practice of these ancient yogic breathing techniques helps increase and strengthen the flow of prana in the body.

We were instructed to add both hatha yoga and pranayamas to our meditation practice. Now instead of just meditation, my routine consisted of hatha yoga, followed by pranayamas, followed by meditation, followed by rest.

During the course, we did this new meditation routine not just two times per day, as was our normal practice, but many times per day—up to six to eight times per day. Doing this increased number of daily meditations was called "rounding," and it was done to deepen and strengthen one's experiences both during, and outside of, meditation.

Normally we only experience three states of consciousness—waking, dream state, and deep sleep. Meditation enables us to experience a fourth state, the transcendental state. This transcendental state is actually the foundation, or structural support, the medium, on which these everyday three states of consciousness exist. It is analogous to the screen in a movie theater. The screen does nothing; it just sits there on the wall, not adding or subtracting from the images projected upon it, and you are unaware of it while the movie is playing. Likewise, you are unaware of the transcendence when the waking or dream states are projected upon it. (In deep sleep you are just unaware, period.) Meditation calms and settles the mind, and thoughts go to their subtlest level until they just drop away and you become aware of the transcendence, just as you would become aware of the movie screen, should the projector stop. And, just as the movie screen does not come into existence when the projector stops, the transcendence does not come into existence when the thoughts stop. It's only that now we are aware of it.

Every time you experience the transcendence during meditation, you bring a little more of its awareness and effects with you when you return to your normal state of wakefulness. It's like dyeing a piece of cloth by dipping it into a dye solution—every time you dip the cloth in and pull it out, a little more of the color is imparted onto the cloth. During practice, the TM-Sidhis are done, or introduced, while in the transcendental state. This means that we must be able to think, to act, while in the transcendental state. How is this possible? While our normal states of consciousness (waking, dreaming, and deep sleep) are mutually exclusive of one another, it is possible to have the experience of each of these three states, not with one another, but with the transcendental state—concurrently, for while the states of waking, dreaming, and deep sleep come and go, the transcendental state does not. It is always there, just under the surface; it is only our awareness of it that comes and goes.

We were spending so much time going in and out of the transcendence during the intensive rounding of the prep course that the transcendental state and wakeful state started to merge so that we could start to feel the calm, still silence of the transcendence while in our normal wakeful state, and, conversely, we could keep some of our thinking awareness with us while in the transcendental state.

The first week of my TM-Sidhi preparatory course was held at a motel in Stuart, Florida. The remainder of my prep course was at a bed-and-breakfast in the middle of a large orange grove in Lake Wales, Florida. The TM organization had rented the whole place for the course. We spent our entire time immersed in meditation. When we weren't meditating, we were watching videotapes of Maharishi explaining the knowledge of meditation. We had our own cooks who prepared vegetarian meals for us, and we only went outside to take short walks to give us some physical activity and exercise. Meditating so much gave us all a spacey kind of feeling, where everything slowed down and we entered into a very relaxed, calm state, both physically and mentally. Stress release intensified, giving our nervous systems the capacity to experience higher states of consciousness. That state of witnessing that I went into on the car ride home from the retreat with Amrit Desai and his teacher, Bapuji, was happening every day and for extended periods of time. When I was actually meditating, the sense of well-being and expansion was overwhelming. It's hard to put into words, but the feeling I had during my meditations was as if my consciousness, my being, expanded to the size of a giant warehouse, and inside of this huge expanse of consciousness was my physical self, meditating in a small space that was about the size of a phone booth situated in a corner of this giant warehouse of consciousness.

The eight weeks of the TM-Sidhi prep course did not have to be completed consecutively. After completing my first week in November of 1977, I went back to Gainesville for two months and then went to Lake Wales to take five more weeks consecutively, starting in January of 1978. I then took another month off and then went back for my seventh and final week of the siddhi prep course at the end of March 1978. I only had to do seven weeks of the prep courses, as I was having very deep meditative experiences and it was determined by the course leaders that I did not need to do an eighth week before starting the actual eight-week siddhi course.

On April 7, 1978, six days after finishing my prep course, I went to the TM center in Livingston Manor, New

York, to start my TM-Sidhi course. The Livingston Manor center was a 460-acre resort in the Catskills. The main residential building had over 250 rooms in addition to dining areas, auditoriums, common areas, and meeting rooms. The grounds were spectacular with forests, rolling green hills, and a large lake. Maharishi wanted men and women separated on the siddhi courses, so Livingston Manor was a men's-only facility. Women did their course at the nearby South Fallsburg, New York facility. Maharishi first introduced the TM-Sidhis program in 1975, but those early courses were only open to TM teachers. In 1977 the course was made available for the first time to meditators who were not TM teachers. My course was the second TM-Sidhi course ever taught to non-teacher meditators. It was originally scheduled to be taught over a consecutive eight-week period. The group before us that had just completed the first meditator TM-Sidhi course (over eight straight weeks) had problems adjusting back to normal life after their course was over. It seemed that people's physiologies had changed so drastically that they were having difficulty coping with everyday life when they got back home. Maharishi thought it best to break up the course so that people's systems could stabilize and not be overly taxed. My course format was changed and taught for two weeks on, then one month off, then two weeks on, and another month off, followed by the final four weeks.

The first thing we learned was how to actually do the siddhi techniques, starting with three sutras. We then learned additional sutras throughout the course, with the final siddhi sutra, the yogic flying, or levitation technique, taught during the last four weeks. One of the siddhis I learned during my first two-week session of the course was the one for super strength, or strength of an elephant. I was always a pretty strong guy.

When my dad was younger, he was a real monster. He had a 22-inch neck, a 54-inch chest, and a 32-inch waist. My dad attributed his strength to doing pull-ups. He had a pull-up bar across his bedroom doorway and did pull-ups every day. When I was little, my dad would hold me up to his pull-up bar so I could do pull-ups. At first I could only hang for a few moments, but eventually I too could do a pull-up. When I was a teenager, my dad put a pull-up bar across my bedroom doorway, and I also started doing pull-ups every day. In high school I had the record for doing the most pull-ups. By college, I was doing a minimum of 120 pull-ups per day. I could do a complete pull-up from a dead hang with Niki on my back. Anyhow, when I started to do the technique for the strength of an elephant, I could feel my body start to get bigger, a lot bigger. Normally during meditation I would feel my consciousness expanding, but not so much my body. If it did feel like my body was expanding, it was only by a little. Now I felt that my body was getting so big that it was going to fill up the entire room. The feeling was so intense that I opened my eyes a bit to take a peek at how big I was. To my surprise, I was the same size. My body was taking up the same amount of space that it always did. I closed my eyes and kept doing the technique.

After lunch that day, I got up to get some tea and then came back to my table. The dining hall was large and seated maybe 150 people at round, eight-person tables. Most people had finished their lunch and left, and there were only about forty of us in the room. Another person from my course and I were the only ones sitting at my table. I picked up my teacup to have a sip of tea when, in an instant, my body shot out in all directions. It was like an explosion. I could feel flames of energy going outward in every direction and filling the room. Although my physical body hadn't changed, I could feel it vibrating tremendously. I quickly set my teacup down on the table so I wouldn't spill it. I heard a loud, really loud, humming, vibrating sound emanating from my entire body. The part of my body that shot out was my consciousness. I could feel that every person and everything in the room was inside of me. People, tables, chairs, dishes, counters—everything. Everything was separate and distinct from me, yet at the same time it was all inside of me, inside of my consciousness. It was all a part of me. My body was shaking, and the noise was deafening. I could barely keep it together. Accompanying these sensations was a feeling of overwhelming joy or bliss, a feeling that no matter what happened to me, nothing would matter; nothing could pull me out of this state. Then, just as quickly as it came, everything stopped and I was back to normal. I looked at the guy across the table, waiting for him to say, "What the hell was that?" I was about to say something, but then I noticed that he was acting as if nothing at all had happened. I didn't say a word. I just excused myself and got up and went to my room. I had to try to figure out what had just happened to me.

I only had a short time back in my room before my afternoon session was to begin. *What happened to me at lunch?* I wasn't sure, but I thought I had had an experience of being enlightened. Why didn't it last? I had always thought that when you become enlightened you stayed enlightened. One of these theories was obviously wrong. Either I did not have an experience of being enlightened, or, if I did, you don't necessarily stay enlightened once you've had the experience. I was pretty sure that I had had an experience of enlightenment, albeit only a small taste that just scratched the surface of a broad continuum of higher states of consciousness that could be included under the umbrella of what is called enlightenment. This experience both verified and clarified so many of the concepts that I had read about over the years. Maharishi had always said that knowledge and experience go hand in hand, and that you need both to progress on the spiritual path. He described it as one hand washing the other. This short experience, which lasted thirty seconds to a minute, helped clear up years of accumulated knowledge. I had had plenty of experiences meditating over the last several years, but nothing anywhere near what I had just experienced. My consciousness had filled an entire room, and everything in the room was inside of, and a part of, me, and yet at the same time everything still had a separateness and individuality of its own. My expanded consciousness had a vibrating, energy-like quality to it. Accompanying this expanded consciousness was a sense of peace and well-being, and a feeling that was much more than just extreme joy or happiness; it was bliss. While happening, it felt like nothing could pull me out of this feeling I was experiencing, an ultimate feeling of non-attachment.

I had read much about bliss and non-attachment, but now I realized how they are both an inseparable part of pure consciousness. Bliss can't be described; it has to be experienced. It's actually less of an experience and more of what an expanded state of consciousness is; a characteristic of the centered state of being. Attachment can be viewed as an emotional bond that connects a person to something else, be it another person, place, or thing, as in: Small children are attached to their mothers and never want to leave their sides; she was attached to that old pair of jeans and didn't want to throw them out; he was attached to his house and didn't want to sell it. Attachment can be viewed even more subtly as anything that grabs your attention, be it looking at a flower or watching a TV show, and attracts your awareness of it, causing a connection or bond. It has been said that attachment is the root cause of suffering, worries, and restlessness, and that if you practice non-attachment, or detachment, you release yourself from these external desires and bonds, and this in turn helps you to reach higher states of consciousness. Some believe non-attachment to mean giving things up, which in the extreme would mean renunciation—giving up the worldly life and leading a holy life. This is not what non-attachment means. Mentally trying to give things up is not really being non-attached; it is just creating an artificial mood of non-attachment. I now knew that real non-attachment is a naturally occurring phenomenon that comes with higher states of consciousness.

During my experience in the dining hall, I had the unshakable realization that my true Self, the "I" of "Who am I?" was just pure, unbounded consciousness. I still had a sense of individuality, but it was not attached to my body or thoughts; it was attached to this overwhelming, vibrat-

ing, all- pervasive consciousness. With this new awareness came an unwavering bliss. The consciousness *was*
bliss, and nothing could pull me out of this state of true
non-attachment. Just a very small part of my awareness
was cognizant of everyone and everything in the room. My
overwhelming awareness was of this bliss consciousness.
Nothing could be more charming or more joyful than this
state of consciousness, nor could anything pull my awareness from it in any significant way. But the reality was that
there was nothing in this room *but* this consciousness. Everything was just an undivided part of this all-pervading
awareness, my awareness, an awareness that was incon-
trovertibly me.

Non-attachment is not renunciation. It is more like
taking things as they naturally come and accepting all—
the good, the bad, and the ugly—with equal joy. Years ago
there was an article in the paper about an Indian guru who
lived on the West Coast and had something like thirty-five
Rolls-Royces. People were giving him a hard time about
having all these extravagant possessions. He said, "Look,
I have a lot of very rich followers, and they like to give me
Rolls-Royces, so I just accept them and drive around in
them, but really, I could care less about them. I'd be just as
happy riding around in an old beat-up Volkswagen or on
a rickety bicycle, but I have the Rolls-Royces so I might as
well just use them and enjoy them." Non-attachment has
nothing to do with giving things up. It's just the way you
naturally relate to things when you have realized, and live
in, that state of who, or what, you truly are.

Maharishi used to talk about the 200 percent value of life. If you lived in a cave in India and meditated your

whole life and became totally enlightened, became one with the universe and totally blissed out, you would have 100 percent of the Absolute, or spiritual aspect of life. If you made millions of dollars and had houses, boats, airplanes, and lived in a mansion with your beautiful family, you would have 100 percent of the relative, or worldly, aspect of life. But life is meant to be lived 200 percent, as these two aspects are not mutually exclusive. You can attain self-realization and live in the world at the same time, thus living and experiencing all that life has to offer.

I determined that I did have a taste of enlightenment, albeit very brief. Although I didn't need it, the experience gave me confirmation that I was on the right path. I finished up my first two weeks of the siddhis course and returned a month later to do my second two weeks. The month after that I was back to Livingston Manor for my final four weeks to learn the technique for flying. Maharishi taught that what keeps us from realizing higher states of consciousness is stress. He stated that stress was actually something that is physically in the nervous system, and that releasing stress was what was necessary to progress on the spiritual path. Meditation not only naturally releases stress, enabling one to experience higher states of consciousness; it also strengthens the nervous system and prevents the negative aspects of stress from building up. The siddhis were meant to hasten the release of stress.

I released a lot of stress during my first four weeks of the course, and I was feeling great, with an overwhelming sense of peace and contentment. I felt really happy no matter what I was doing or even when I was doing nothing at all.

I was excited to learn the flying technique. I don't remember exactly how many people were on my siddhi course with me, maybe twenty. We learned the sutra for flying, but when I did it nothing happened. I felt good, as I did in all my meditations, but I did not lift off the floor. I thought that I would just float up, like Aladdin on his magic carpet, and fly around the room, but I just sat there cross-legged on the floor. A couple of the guys started hopping around, their bodies jerking up off the ground, but no one was staying in the air, and no one was defying the laws of gravity. We practiced the flying technique twice a day for the entire four weeks. As the four-week course progressed, more people started to jerk up off the floor and hop around the room, but at the end, some of us, myself included, never got off the ground. I never moved an inch. I was a little disappointed that I didn't levitate but not *that* disappointed. I didn't learn meditation for stress release, or to gain better health, or to obtain super-normal abilities. I learned to meditate so as to experience higher states of consciousness, to attain enlightenment, to just figure out what was really going on. While I hadn't attained enlightenment after four years of meditating and completion of my siddhi course, I did have a brief experience of enlightenment, and my consciousness was definitely at a new level.

CHAPTER 9

Back to Gainesville

After completing the siddhi course, I returned to Gainesville to continue my quest for enlightenment. I now thought I had everything I needed to complete the task. My daily meditation routine had gone from meditating for forty minutes a day (twenty minutes in the morning and afternoon) to three hours a day (one and a half hours in the morning and afternoon), including a daily hatha yoga routine that was done before each meditation. My whole schedule revolved around meditating. I told my friends that if they wanted to do something early in the morning, I needed to know the night before. Any time was fine, just as long as I had advance notice. If they wanted to do something at, say, 5:00 a.m., no problem. I would just set my alarm for 3:00 a.m. In the afternoon, no matter where I was or what I was doing, I would always slip off to a room or private spot to do my afternoon meditation.

I hadn't done any drugs or had anything to drink since I had started my siddhi course nine months prior. During my first weeks at home, when I was on a two-month break following my first week of the prep course, my friends would try to get me to smoke pot with them. I hung with a pretty crazy crowd, and everyone was always getting high. I told them I wasn't going to get high because of the meditation course I was taking. After a week or so they stopped asking me to get high and just handed me the joint to pass when we were all sitting around together. After a few more weeks, they didn't even pass me the joint; they just passed it around me. After that, they started telling people in the room not to blow smoke anywhere near me, as I did not get high. Finally they stopped smoking pot around me altogether. Either they would go someplace else, or I would leave the room. I just did not want to breathe any smoke. Drinking was a little easier. I just didn't drink. We would all go out to the bars together and everything would be the same. I was just as crazy as ever, dancing and partying, only now, while everyone else was drinking alcohol, I was drinking water or club soda.

Although it wasn't my plan, I never did drugs again after I stopped taking them to do the siddhi course. I got high for one reason—I liked it. I liked being high. The situation now was that I was always high, naturally high from meditating. And I'm not talking about just feeling good. I was at a whole different level. I got higher from meditating than I ever did from doing drugs, and when I wasn't meditating, I was going in and out of the witnessing state. I'd be driving down the road in my car and the next thing I know I'd be driving through myself, through my consciousness. Everything was just unbounded awareness. *I* was unbounded awareness. The same thing would happen when I was sitting or walking around. I'd be having a moment of inner stillness and the next thing I knew, everything had slowed down and I, and everything around me, was in this mass of consciousness, my consciousness. I kept going in and out of this state where everything was like a dream, except I wasn't dreaming. I was totally awake with 100 percent mental clarity. It was happening so often that I was becoming unaware of whether it was happening or not. I had always known that one day I would stop doing drugs forever, as I believed that doing drugs would slow down and hinder my spiritual advancement. I just didn't know that it would be in November of 1977, at the age of twenty-seven.

A few weeks after finishing my siddhi course, I decided to have a couple of beers. That night I couldn't get to sleep, and the next day I felt terrible, and I slept lousily for the next couple of nights. Several weeks later I had another couple of beers, and again I couldn't get to sleep, and I felt lousy the next day, and I didn't sleep well for the next couple of nights. For some reason, I just could not drink. I think that my system had changed so much from all the intensive meditating I had done on my siddhi course that my body could no longer handle alcohol. Besides not feeling well, I just did not want to have any alcohol in my system. So, for all intents and purposes, I also stopped drinking in November of 1977, at the age of twenty-seven.

For as long as I could remember, I had been a coffee drinker. My aunt Flossie was my favorite aunt and she drank her coffee black—no cream; no sugar. I wanted to be like her, so, in 1954, at the age of four, I started drinking my coffee black. I know it sounds crazy, but my parents had let me drink coffee when I was even younger than four, the age when I started drinking my coffee black—no cream; no sugar. Into adulthood, I drank coffee every day, and I really enjoyed the taste. I'd buy whole beans from Colombia or Costa Rica, grind them fresh every day, and brew my coffee in a professional machine. Several months after finishing my siddhi course, I was having my morning cup of coffee when I started to feel like I was on speed. I felt anxious and jittery and could not relax. I attributed this feeling to my system changing from all the meditation that I was doing. That was the last time I had a cup of coffee.

Maharishi wanted meditators who did the TM-Sidhi Program to receive as much knowledge as they could about Transcendental Meditation and higher states of consciousness, and during our eight-week siddhi course we were shown Transcendental Meditation teacher training tapes. Even though we were not going to be TM teachers, Maharishi thought it important for us to have this knowledge. After finishing the siddhi course, I had had so many experiences, and had so much knowledge on meditation and the benefits it could provide, that I wanted to spread the word to the world. I'd talk to anyone who would listen—family, friends, even strangers in bars.

I soon came to realize that most people weren't that interested in meditation or spiritual pursuits. If they were interested, it was only mildly. After a few months I stopped bringing up the subject. If it came up in conversation, or if someone asked, I'd be happy to talk about it ad nauseam. Otherwise, I just left it alone.

Several months after finishing the TM-Sidhi course, I was doing the flying technique part of my program when suddenly I started hopping around the room. I was sitting on the floor with my legs folded in a full lotus position when my body jerked off the ground. It was quite unexpected. I wasn't trying to lift off the floor; I was just sitting, very relaxed, in a cross-legged position doing my sutra when, with no warning, my body jerked up off the ground. The movement wasn't any different from me intentionally using my muscles to jerk up and hop forward, except that I wasn't trying to hop. I was simply doing my mental technique. Over the next few years I continued to sporadically hop around while practicing my flying sutra. As my knowledge and experience grew, I started to have no interest in levitating, and I just stopped coming off the ground when I did my flying technique. I continued practicing all the Patanjali's yoga sutras that I had learned on my siddhi course, including my flying sutra, but only for the purpose of realizing higher states of consciousness. I had no interest whatsoever in obtaining any yogic powers.

CHAPTER 10

Some Interesting Experiences

Even though I had no interest in obtaining yogic abilities or powers, I do believe that over the years certain things I did or became inexplicably aware of came as a direct result of my meditating and practicing the TM-Sidhis. These are a few of the more memorable events:

After completing my siddhi course, I returned to Florida and had a very strange dream that seemed to go on all night. In it, I tried over and over to call Benjie, my roommate during law school and one of my best friends, but I could not do it. I kept fumbling with the phone, unable to pick it up, hold it in my hand, or dial the numbers. The next morning I got up, meditated, and had started to make my breakfast when Benjie called to tell me that he had tried over and over to call me the night before from Miami. He was with friends, and they were so high they kept dialing the wrong number and couldn't get through.

A year or two after completing the siddhis, I was down at the Jersey Shore, at my parents' house, and a bunch of us were playing horseshoes on the beach. The sand at the Jersey Shore is really soft, and during the course of play we lost one of the horseshoes in the sand. We were all looking for it, but it was not to be found. We started an organized search pattern where we crisscrossed the area, digging our toes into the sand to feel for it, but we had no luck. Suddenly, a thought popped into my head: *This is stupid.* I picked up one of the three remaining horseshoes, took a few steps, lifted it over my head, and plunged it into the sand as hard as I could—one time—*clink!* I had struck the lost horseshoe.

In September of 1979 I was asked by a friend if I would meet with his realtor to show him a piece of property my friend wanted to list for sale. My friend was living in Tampa and the property was located twenty miles outside of Gainesville, so I said okay. The realtor picked me up early in the morning and we drove out in his car. The property, about forty-five acres, was undeveloped, with just a small trailer on it. Except for a few trees, the land was mostly covered in chest-high weeds. Gainesville is warm in September, and all I had on were shorts, a T-shirt, and sandals. We were walking around the property when suddenly something grabbed my left foot and started biting me. It was biting hard, and it really hurt. I lifted my leg and shook the creature off. I couldn't see what it was, as the weeds were so thick, but whatever it was, it was heavy. I parted the weeds with my hands and looked down and there it was—an eastern diamondback rattlesnake. The largest, most venomous, most deadly snake in North America. The snake with the largest fangs of any rattlesnake species in the world. This one was about five feet long, and it had just given me everything it had. It didn't just bite me; it gnawed on me. I turned to the realtor and said, "Get me to the hospital," and we started to walk toward his car, which was about 100 yards away. I took two steps and my lips and lower face went numb. By the time we got to the car, I could barely walk and the realtor had to help me get in.

As we drove toward Shands Hospital, I closed my eyes to meditate. One of the sutras we learned on the TM-Sidhi course was for healing your body, and I thought if I could do this, I would be okay. As I started to meditate, I felt myself leave my body. This wasn't my consciousness expanding; this was my consciousness leaving. I got scared and stopped meditating. A few moments later, I started to have difficulty breathing. I thought I might actually die. This fear didn't last long, for as I started to contemplate my impending death, strangely, a stillness and acceptance came over me that it would be okay. I was going to die, but everything would be okay.

The hospital was about a half-hour away, and cell phones were not around yet. We drove a couple of miles and stopped at a small country store to use their phone to call the hospital to tell them what had happened and that I was coming in. By the time we got there, I could barely move. I was helped out of the car and put onto a gurney.

In the emergency room they wanted to collect my personal information, but I could barely speak. In a whisper I told them that my wallet was in my back pocket. I didn't have the physical ability to get it out, so they rolled me over slightly to remove it. The surgeon surprised me by asking, "Where's the snake?" When I told him I hadn't brought it, he pulled out a chart with pictures of about thirty different kinds of snakes on it and asked me to identify the one that had bitten me, but they all looked the same. I told him it was an eastern diamondback rattle-snake. Having lived in North Florida for six years, I had seen them before. I was sure.

When I got to the emergency room, my fear of death returned. On the car ride in, I was resigned to the fact that I might die and there was nothing I could do about it. Now I was in a premier trauma hospital, sur-rounded by top-notch medical personnel who might actu-ally be able to help me. I just wanted them to do it and do it quickly. With an IV tube in my arm delivering two vials of antivenin, I was being wheeled to the surgical intensive care unit when I asked, "What's the worst that will hap-pen to me?"

Walking beside my gurney, the doctor answered, "The worst that could happen is that you could die."

Venom from an eastern diamondback rattlesnake causes great pain and also tremendous tissue damage. Typically, a bite requires surgery to cut out and repair the area around it. They had wheeled me into surgical inten-sive care anticipating that they would have to cut out part of my foot. All my vital signs were off—my blood pres-sure, my pulse, my respiration—everything. My left foot was swelling, and I had eleven puncture wounds in three toes. The pain was excruciating. If I moved my leg even a little, I thought I was going to throw up.

"I'll give you something for the pain," the doctor said.

"No," I answered. "I don't want to take anything."

He hesitated. "You should take something or this will be unbearable."

"No," I said, though my voice was whispery and weak. "If I'm going to die, I want to have total awareness, full consciousness when I go"

He shook his head, but said, "Okay."

Still barely able to speak, I told him that I knew this very intensive meditation program that I thought would make me better, but if I did it, it would slow my entire system to almost nothing and I didn't want to mess myself up. Having already dismissed me as a bit strange, he said, "It's fine to do that, but I don't think it's going to help you." As he turned to walk out the door, I closed my eyes.

I had been doing my advanced meditation program for over a year, spending an hour and a half every morning and an hour and a half every afternoon doing Hatha yoga, pranayamas, meditation, and the siddhis. There, in the hospital, I couldn't do my yoga or pranayamas, as I could barely move, so I did my meditation and the siddhis. As I let go and started to meditate, I felt my awareness expand and my body disappear into that expanding awareness. I dissolved into a vast expanse of unbounded consciousness. About an hour passed in what seemed just a few minutes, and as I let my body stabilize, the doctor came back in to check on me. He examined me and then walked over to talk to Benjie, who was waiting just outside my door. I had given the hospital his number as a local person to call. Benjie asked the doctor how I was doing, and the doctor told him that I would be fine. He told him that I hadn't been bitten by a rattlesnake. He said he had just checked all my vital signs and everything was stable, and that it was absolutely impossible for anyone to stabilize this quickly after being bitten by a rattlesnake.

I knew he was wrong. It was a rattlesnake that had bitten me. The doctor returned to my room later that afternoon to examine me once again. My left foot was now swollen to the size of a football and the pain was intense. The area around my toes where I was bitten had turned yellow, and the skin on top of my foot had turned black, with black lines starting to creep up my leg. The doctor took one look at this and conceded that I had definitely been bitten by an eastern diamondback rattlesnake, although he couldn't explain why all my vital signs were stable. He took out a black marker and made a line on my skin at the top of the blackness that was going up my leg. They continued to check on me and mark the blackness as it progressed. It eventually stopped around my knee.

I never took anything for the pain from the snakebite. All I got were three or four vials of the antivenin. The doctor had originally told me that I would be in the hospital for up to two weeks. I was in for forty-eight hours. Two weeks after I was released from the hospital, I went to see the doctor at his office for a follow-up. Just to prove a point, I walked into his office without my crutches and tried to walk without a limp, even though my foot was still killing me. He examined my foot and leg. There was still a lot of discoloration, but he said I would be okay. He then told me that I was the only person he had ever treated for an eastern diamondback rattlesnake bite that didn't require surgery to repair the tissue damage.

In 1981 I drove to South Carolina to visit a friend who lived in the western part of the state. My friend lived out in the country and one day we had to drive into town to pick up some things he needed. We spent a good part of the day getting everything he needed, and before heading back, we stopped at a food store to get some stuff for dinner. It was a long drive, so I asked if he wouldn't mind driving so I could meditate on the ride back, otherwise I would have to meditate when we got back to his house and I wouldn't be able to eat until really late. He said okay, so he drove and I meditated. As I was meditating, I had this really strong premonition that we were going to be involved in a horrible car accident. This premonition was so strong and so intense that I was going to stop meditating and ask my friend to pull over so I could drive. I thought this was just crazy and that we were not going to be in an accident, so I just kept meditating and let him drive. Ten minutes after I was done meditating, my friend pulled into his very long, gravel driveway, going really fast, and ran over and killed Rocky, who was waiting at his house for me to return and ran out when he saw my car coming.

Moving forward a few years, and on a much lighter note, in 1994 I was walking downstairs after doing my morning meditation, and I had this thought that it would be great if Disney released *Snow White and the Seven Dwarfs*, the 1937 Disney classic that had never been released on video. We had four young kids at the time and I thought it would be really fun if we could all watch this movie together. As I sat down for breakfast, I opened the morning paper and turned to the entertainment section:

"Disney to release *Snow White and the Seven Dwarfs* this week for the first time on VHS."

This sort of thing wasn't new to me, and it didn't start happening after I did the TM-Sidhi program, or even after I started meditating. When I was a sophomore at North Carolina State University, I gave my mom a call. It was 1969, and we got to talking about Vietnam. I had a lot of friends who were serving, and my mom didn't want me to go.

"Don't worry about it," I said. "I'm not going to have to go."

"What do you mean?" she said. "How do you know that?"

It was November 30, and the government had plans to start the draft lottery the next day. They were going to randomly pick 366 days, one for each day of the year, including one for February 29th for leap years. Men were going to be called up for service in the order that their birthdays were picked.

"I'm going to get number 365," I told her. "I will never have to go."   On December 1st, 1969, the 365th day drawn in the Selective Service System Lottery was February 26, my birthday.

CHAPTER 11

Is God in That Bottle Cap?

In 1982 Niki and I got married and moved to New Jersey. Two years later we had our first child, our daughter, Carly. Two of my best friends had just had kids, and we all thought it would be fun to live near one another as our families grew, so we moved to Charleston, South Carolina, to live near my college roommate Joe, and his family, as did our other college roommate, Jimmy, and his family. I took a job selling commercial real estate and settled into suburban family life. In addition to meditating, I was still doing T'ai Chi every day and taking four weeks of T'ai Chi teacher training classes every year. I had taught T'ai Chi in New York City and Philadelphia, and at Princeton University and the University of Florida, and I decided to offer classes in Charleston through the YMCA and, later, through a wellness program at Roper Hospital.

Teaching at the Y gave me membership privileges, so at lunchtime three days a week I would go to their West Ashley facility to swim laps. Not much socializing goes on when you swim laps, but several of us were regulars and we would strike up conversations in the locker room. One guy I swam with, I believe his name was Dan, was a Christian minister at a local church. I told him that I wasn't much of a churchgoer, but I did meditate a few hours each day. We talked fairly regularly, and he'd always tell me to come to church as it was important, and I'd say, "No, meditation is my church."

One afternoon as we were leaving after our swim, he started in again with trying to get me to go to church. As we got to our cars, I looked down and lying on the ground by the edge of the parking lot was a bottle cap. I pointed to it and said, "Dan, is God in that bottle cap?" He looked at me with a smile, waiting for the punch line. I said, "No, really, is God in that bottle cap?" He saw that I was serious and just looked at me. I didn't wait for a reply. "If God is everywhere, is he in that bottle cap, or is he everywhere, just not in that bottle cap? How about the bullet that shot Kennedy? Was God in the bullet that shot Kennedy, or is he everywhere, just not in the bullet that shot Kennedy and not in that bottle cap? If God is everywhere, then he has to be in everything; he has to be the ultimate building block of the physical universe."

I kept going. "A thousand years ago people thought that the smallest thing in the world was a molecule. There was a molecule of gold, a molecule of silver, a molecule of dirt. Then, as science got more sophisticated, people thought that the smallest thing in the world was an atom. There was nothing smaller than an atom. Then they said no, the smallest things in the world are subatomic particles—protons, neutrons, and electrons. Then they said no, the smallest things in the world are quarks. Okay, now you can imagine the smallest thing in the world. Go ahead.

Imagine the smallest thing in the world. Got it? Now cut it in half. No matter how small something is, you can always imagine cutting it in half. So the smallest thing in the world, the ultimate building block of the entire physical universe, can't have any mass. It can't have any weight. It's just pure nothingness, but it is something and you can give it a name. You can call it energy. You can call it consciousness. You can call it nature. You can call it God. You can call it anything you want, but it is the ultimate building block of the entire universe, even thoughts.

"Now, see your finger?" And I pointed to his finger. "There's nothing different in your finger than what's in that bottle cap. It's just different combinations of the same stuff. So now, are you Dan, this person, or are you this stuff that you are made of, this pure consciousness, this nothingness? Well, on one level you're Dan, but on another level you are this stuff that you are made up of. It's like a wooden chair. At one level it's a chair, but on another level it's wood. Okay, now imagine you're this pure consciousness, and you really are this pure consciousness, this stuff that you're made up of, and you know that you're made up of it and you are it. Not just on an intellectual level, but on a real level, and you can think and function from this level. You could hold out your hand," and I held my hand out, palm up, "and you could say *apple*, and there is an apple in your hand. Not a fake apple, but a real apple, because an apple is made of pure consciousness; you are pure consciousness, and you can function at this level of pure consciousness. Or you could go—*Water into wine. Blind man see. Dead man rise.* But if you did that, people would say, 'Oh my god, you're God!' And you would say, 'No, no, I'm not God. Well yes, kind of. Well no. Well we're the same but different. Well, he's the father, I'm the son'"—I stopped talking. I had captured Dan's full attention and could tell from his expression that he had never heard anything like this before, and he was just trying to take it all in and process it.

Without waiting for a response, I said: "See you later, I got to get back to work," and I got into my car and drove off. I don't remember seeing much of Dan after that. We never spoke about the talk I had had with him. He stopped coming to the Y, and someone told me he quit the ministry.

CHAPTER 12

Being a Lawyer

I didn't make much money selling commercial real estate in Charleston, and after six years, two more kids (Troy and Maddie), and a fourth on the way, Niki said, "You have got to make some money. You need to be a lawyer." Even though I went to law school, I never really wanted to be a lawyer. I had opened an antique store, a gift shop, a pizza restaurant, taught T'ai Chi, and sold commercial real estate—anything except practice law. We talked it over and decided that if I was going to practice law, the best place would probably be back in the South Jersey/Philadelphia area. It had been fifteen years since I had graduated from law school and tax school, and I hadn't thought about law or opened a law book once during that time. After graduating from the University of Florida Law School, I took and passed the Florida bar exam, but I never took the bar exams for New Jersey and Pennsylvania; exams I would have to take, and pass, if I was to practice law in those states. To pass those exams, I would need to take a bar review course that covered both states, and do a lot of studying. For this endeavor I would need to be 100-percent focused, so in January of 1991 I left my pregnant wife and three kids in South Carolina and went to New Jersey to take a six-week bar review course.

I stayed at my parents' house in New Jersey and spent my days studying. Five nights a week I attended a bar review course. I was one of the older persons taking the course, as most of my classmates had just graduated from law school. Toward the end, we all took a practice exam that was given nationwide to all who attended the review course. I scored in the top 2 percent in the country. Two weeks after my course ended, I took my bar exams for Pennsylvania and New Jersey, three days of all-day testing. Passing both, I was now a member of the Pennsylvania, New Jersey, and Florida bars.

Now I needed a job. A friend of mine who had attended law school with me in Gainesville had his own practice in Tampa. His practice was limited solely to motor vehicle accidents, and he was making a bundle. He agreed to take me in and show me the business, so Niki and I packed up the kids and we moved to Tampa, Florida, for four months. My friend had a volume practice, and during that time I learned the ropes and settled fifty cases with insurance companies. Also during that time, Niki gave birth to our fourth child, our son Dylan. Six weeks after Dylan was born we packed up again, now the six of us, and moved to West Chester, Pennsylvania, so that I could start my own law practice.

As did my lawyer friend in Tampa, I limited my practice solely to motor vehicle accidents. Almost all of my cases were accidents that happened in Philadelphia. We picked West Chester as a place to live, as another one of my best friends, Bill, lived there, and it wasn't too far from Philly. I again decided to teach T'ai Chi classes, so I contacted the Upper Main Line YMCA and started teaching classes there. I also started taking T'ai Chi classes one night a week in Philadelphia, studying with Maggie Newman, another of Cheng Man-ch'ing's senior students. As always, I meditated every day. Sadly, after living in West Chester for a little less than a year, my friend Bill died very suddenly and unexpectedly from a brain aneurism. I have dozens of good friends, but only six whom I consider to be my very best friends, friends who are like family to me. Bill was one of those friends.

CHAPTER 13

Learning Qigong

With Bill gone, we decided to move back to Haddonfield. I stopped teaching T'ai Chi, but I kept up with my classes with Maggie Newman in Philadelphia. In 1996, one of the women in our class told everyone that she had just taken a qigong class with a qigong master from China, and that it was really great and we should check it out. I signed up for the next class. Qigong is an ancient Chinese natural healing and health care system that integrates physical postures and movement, breathing techniques, and focused awareness to gather, circulate, and store qi (chi), the life force, or vital-energy, that flows through all things in the universe. Like T'ai Chi, qigong balances the qi in the body thus harmonizing the body/mind/spirit connection. There is archaeological evidence suggesting that the first forms of qigong are linked to ancient shamanic meditative practices dating back 7,000 years.

The qigong class was taught by FaXiang Hou, a master of medical qigong and traditional Chinese medicine who had recently immigrated to the United States from Mainland China. Master Hou was a fifth-generation qigong master, and the style he taught was his family's style, a powerful form of healing qigong called Ching Loong San Dian Xue Mi Gong Fa (Green Dragon and Three Secret Points). In addition to studying with his father, Master Hou had also studied with five other accomplished masters in China. Master Hou's qigong used specific body positions, movements, and breathing techniques to move the qi with the mind, through certain pathways in the body. With the very first exercise I learned, I could actually feel the qi flowing, like an energy or warmth traveling through my body. I really couldn't believe how much I was feeling the qi. It wasn't just a trickle that I felt: It was more like a freight train.

I have been studying with Master Hou now for over twenty-two years, and I am one of his senior students. In addition to taking twenty weeks of class a year, I try to do a little qigong every day on my own. Doing qigong is like meditation to me, a meditation in which I feel the qi (prana) flowing continuously through my body. The actual feeling I have doing qigong is this: I feel my physical body dissolve, and I am just an unbounded mass of consciousness or energy, then, inside this unbounded expanse, I feel the qi flowing in specific pathways as directed by the actual qigong exercise that I am doing. It is like energy moving inside of energy, qi (prana) moving inside of unmoving consciousness.

CHAPTER 14

Learning Sudarshan Kriya

In June of 1996 I got a call from Ilene, Niki's friend from college who had introduced me to Transcendental Meditation back in 1974. We had not heard from Ilene in years. She called to tell me that she had been seeing this Indian guru, a Sri Sri Ravi Shankar, who used to be a follower of Maharishi Mahesh Yogi. Guruji, as Sri Sri Ravi Shankar was known, started this worldwide organization called The Art of Living (AOL) and taught a rhythmic, breathing-based meditative technique called Sudarshan Kriya. Ilene told me that I definitely had to check this guy out and learn the Sudarshan Kriya.

I trusted Ilene's opinion on these matters, so the next day I found a number for an Art of Living center in North Jersey and gave them a call. I told them I wanted to sign up to learn their Sudarshan Kriya. They said, "No problem," as they taught these courses fairly regularly and had one coming up soon. I asked if Ravi Shankar would be at the course, and they said, "No, he is never at beginner courses, where the Sudarshan Kriya is taught, he is only at advanced courses." They advised me to sign up for a beginner course and then later on take an advanced course, where I could be with him.

I said, "No, I want to take a beginner course when he will be there and I can meet him."

They said, "That's not possible, he hasn't been at a beginner course in years."

I said, "That's okay, just take my name and number and call me when he's at a beginner course." I could hear the resignation in their voice as they obligingly took my name and number over the phone.

The very next day I got a call back from the Art of Living. They said, "You're not going to believe it, but a beginner course just got scheduled for California, and Sri Sri Ravi Shankar will be there. It's a combination beginner and advanced course, where you can take the beginner course and be with Guruji for all his talks."

I said, "Sign me up."

Six weeks later I flew to Santa Monica, California, to learn Sudarshan Kriya and meet Guruji.

The course I signed up for was one week long. All of us on the beginner course (now called the Happiness Program) stayed at a really swanky motel in Santa Monica that was right across the street from the beach. Our Sudarshan Kriya class was small, maybe ten of us plus two teachers, and it was taught in one of the motel's rooms. The advanced course, which had several hundred people, was taught a few blocks away at the Santa Monica Civic Auditorium. This was also where Sri Sri Ravi Shankar held his talks. Our class was taught during the day, and in the evening we would all go to hear Guruji speak. Sometimes we would also go to his afternoon talks, and one day after one of his afternoon talks, our small group got to meet him personally.

Seeing Guruji and hearing him speak was really a moving experience for me. It was almost as if he was from another planet, not in the way of being like an alien, but more like there were us, the people of the Earth, and him. He didn't seem to be speaking about things he had learned or heard from some outside source, but rather things he had experienced and come to know internally. Spiritual, higher-states-of-consciousness stuff that I had been reading about for years and knew somewhat from my experiences, he seemed to be living. I was just happy to be in his presence.

I really didn't know what to expect from doing the Sudarshan Kriya, as Ilene did not tell me anything about it. She just said I should learn it. Sudarshan means proper seeing or vision. Kriya is an exercise that purifies or cleanses. Sudarshan Kriya is a purifying breathing practice whereby one receives a proper vision of one's true self. The rhythmic breathing patterns of Sudarshan Kriya harmonize the rhythms of the body and emotions, and bring them in tune with the rhythms of nature. Sudarshan Kriya is a breathing-based meditation that calms and relaxes the mind, and helps rid the system of stress, thus allowing one to experience the transcendental, pure consciousness state.

We learned a couple of breathing techniques, and then the class did the Kriya all together. I was as blown away as I had been when I first learned to meditate some twenty-two years earlier. My body seemed to just dissolve as my consciousness expanded in all directions with no

perceivable boundaries. With this expansion of consciousness came an overwhelming sense of joyful contentment,
a perfect contentment that nothing could improve upon as
everything was as it should be. I told the teachers leading
the course what a great experience I had had doing the
Kriya, and then they told me—we hadn't done the Kriya;
we had only done the preliminary breathing exercises that
are done right before the start of the Sudarshan Kriya. We
were going to learn the Sudarshan Kriya the next day. I
couldn't believe it. If this was my experience from doing
just the preliminary breathing exercises, what could I possibly expect from doing the actual Kriya? I'd find out the
next day.

The next day we all learned and did the Sudarshan
Kriya, and yes, it was great. But what do I mean when
I say it was great? All my spiritual experiences, be they
from meditating, doing the TM-Sidhi program, Sudarshan Kriya, T'ai Chi, qigong, or from doing nothing whatsoever, have the same flavor, as they are all awarenesses of
the same transcendental state, that ever-existent state of
consciousness lying just under the surface of the waking,
dreaming, and deep-sleep states. They are all flavors of a
flavorless pure consciousness that is without attributes,
yet, at the same time, has characteristics, unexpoundable
characteristics, of stillness, peace, and unbounded contentment.

I finished up my Art of Living Sudarshan Kriya
course and flew back to New Jersey. I really enjoyed the
Kriya and decided to make it a part of my daily program
by incorporating it into my Transcendental Meditation
and TM-Sidhi routine. I am careful about protecting the

integrity of my meditation techniques by not mixing them, and that was easy to do in this case. The Sudarshan Kriya is a breathing technique that could be considered a highly specific form of pranayama. Included in, and a part of, my daily TM-Sidhi program was a nonproprietary ten-minute pranayama practice. What I decided to do was to substitute my twenty-minute daily Sudarshan Kriya breathing technique for my ten minutes of pranayamas that I did as part of my morning siddhi program. I found it to be a perfect fit.

There were two variations of the Sudarshan Kriya that we learned on my course. One was a twenty-minute daily home practice that you do on your own, and the other was a longer version that you do once a week with a group led by an Art of Living teacher. Philadelphia had an Art of Living teacher, so I went once a week to do the long Kriya with a local group. Doing the longer weekly group Kriya had a slightly different flavor than my daily individual Sudarshan Kriya practice, and for the next fifteen years I rarely missed attending this weekly group practice.

Meditation techniques are just that and nothing more—techniques—techniques that help facilitate the experience of the transcendence. They are not creating anything. They don't create higher states of consciousness. The absolute, all-pervading pure consciousness is always there; it is only our awareness of it that comes and goes. I explained it like this to a friend of mine who was sitting with me in my kitchen when he asked about meditation. I pointed to a large clock on my kitchen wall and asked him if he heard the clock ticking. He said no. I said the clock is silent and never makes any noise, but one time, during the middle of the night, I came downstairs to the kitchen to get a glass of water. There was dead silence in the house, and I heard the clock ticking! I couldn't believe it. I thought the clock was totally silent but I was wrong; it always made noise, but it was just so faint that you could only hear it in the absolute stillness of the night.

I asked, "When did the clock start ticking?"

My friend started to nod his head.

"Meditation is like that. It doesn't create an experience, it just settles the mind and body, thus allowing the silent awareness to be perceived."

While meditation techniques are so important in helping to realize, and become established in higher states of consciousness, performing them is not the only way to do so, as the experience of a higher state of consciousness can happen to anyone at any time, and for no apparent reason at all. I have found that sometimes the place I'm in can cause transcending or bring about witnessing, such as a church, temple, or monastery—or a mountaintop, forest, or countryside; any place where I can find a moment of stillness.

Several years ago, Niki and I took the kids to Costa Rica for a family vacation. We were on the Nicoya Peninsula, sitting outside on some rocks and waiting for the ferry to take us back to Puntarenas and our flight home, when I felt myself go into a very strong state of witnessing. My thirteen-year-old son Dylan was perched on a rock next to me. All of a sudden Dylan said to me in a somewhat panicked voice, "Something is happening to me."

I asked, "What's happening?"

He said, "I don't know." He sounded really concerned and a bit unnerved.

I asked, "What's going on, tell me what's happening."

He said, "I'm feeling something."

I asked, "What is it?"

He said, "I don't know."

I said, "Explain to me what you are feeling."

He said, "My body feels like it's getting bigger, and everything around me is weird and different." I knew exactly what was happening; he was experiencing the same thing I was.

I told him, "You're okay. You're having a feeling that happens when you meditate. It's called transcending, and it can make you feel like you're watching or witnessing everything around you in a strange way. It's really a nice experience. Just enjoy it."

He was a bit scared and said, "I don't like it. Make it stop."

I told him, "I can't make it stop. You just have to go with it."

He complained for a while, and eventually the feeling stopped and he returned to his normal state.

I found it very interesting that something I experienced all the time, something I found so enjoyable, happened to my son and he did not like it at all. In fact, he was a little afraid. This is one reason why it is so important for knowledge and experience to go hand in hand. You need to know what is happening and what you are experiencing. Back in the 1950s and '60s, the CIA did secret LSD experiments on unsuspecting American civilians and military personnel. People were unknowingly given LSD, and they freaked out. They had no idea what was happening to them and thought they were going crazy. If the victims of these unconscionable experiments had known they had been given LSD, and that LSD was the cause of what they were experiencing, they more than likely could have kept their composure. I was witness to this a few times during my past drug use. I had never done LSD, but I had done psilocybin mushrooms and peyote, and I smoked some very powerful marijuana. I would get high, really high, and I enjoyed every minute of it, but I never forgot that I was doing drugs, so no matter what happened, I just sat back and enjoyed the ride. Occasionally one of my friends getting high with me would start to freak out and panic. They had forgotten they were doing drugs. I would tell them, "It's okay, you're just doing peyote (or whatever), and everything you're feeling is because of the drugs and it's okay; just sit back and enjoy it, you're perfectly okay; it's just the drugs."

Meditation and higher states of consciousness are always pleasant and enjoyable, but it can be alarming to feel and experience new sensations and not understand why. I met a young woman at a party recently who was from Paris, France. She knew I was into meditation and wanted to know what it was all about. As we were talking, I was telling her about my experiences of transcending and witnessing when I was a child. She said, "Oh my God." She had had the same thing happen to her as a child, but thought something was the matter with her. Her parents were going through a divorce and they thought that she was having some type of breakdown, and they sent her to see a psychiatrist. Unfortunately, the psychiatrist had no idea what was going on and couldn't help. Even though her experiences of transcending had stopped many years ago, the young woman now felt relieved to finally understand what it was that had happened to her and know it was nothing bad.

CHAPTER 15

The Guru Comes to Visit

Several months after I finished my Art of Living basic course, Sri Sri Ravi Shankar came to Philadelphia to give a public talk. At that time, when Guruji traveled to various cities to give talks, he would stay at the homes of people who were involved with his organization. Niki and I had a fairly good-sized house only six miles from Philadelphia, and we were lucky enough to have Guruji stay with us for two nights. When Guruji arrived at our house, he brought an entourage of about forty people; members of the Art of Living who were travelling with him. It was late in the afternoon when they arrived and Azah, one of Guruji's closer followers, wanted to know what we were having for dinner. I told him I didn't know. I really hadn't thought about dinner, and I definitely had no idea that Guruji would be coming with forty people.

Azah just said, "Take me to the kitchen, and let's see what you have."

Niki and I are foodies, and even though we hadn't shopped for dinner for fifty, we had a pretty well-stocked kitchen, especially in the spice department. Azah started going through our cupboards, pulling out spices, rice, beans, whatever he could find. From our refrigerator, he took out all the vegetables we had. Azah was like a general: He just took charge. He recruited some of Guruji's entourage to start chopping vegetables while he started throwing things together. When he was done, there was dinner. Not just dinner, but a gourmet feast for fifty. I had no idea that the stuff we just had lying around our kitchen could make such a tasty meal.

The people who were the most impressed with Guruji during his stay with us were our four kids. They all thought that Guruji was the nicest person they had ever met. Dylan, our youngest, had just turned five. He didn't quite get the name "Guruji," so he called Sri Sri "Super-ji." We all did a group meditation in our living room that first night, and Dylan wanted to join in, so for twenty or thirty minutes he sat silently with us, on the floor with his eyes closed and his legs crossed in a lotus position. Several people commented that they had never seen anyone so young sit so quietly for such a long meditation. I wanted to take a picture of Dylan with Guruji, and I asked him to go sit next to Sri Sri. Guruji was sitting in a chair, and Dylan sat at his feet, in a full lotus position. Guruji leaned over and helped him into the chair. As my son sat with Guruji's arm around him, I snapped the picture that I still have today.

We gave Guruji our bedroom so that he would have his own bathroom and more privacy. To ensure that privacy, we swept the bedroom for children each night, as some of our kids would hide under our bed to be with him. It wasn't that surreptitious, as they were all giggling and laughing. That first night, I found myself alone in our bedroom with Guruji, making sure he had everything he needed for the night. This was actually quite rare, as Guruji always seemed to be surrounded by many of his followers. Guruji, who I believed to be one of the great living spiritual masters, looked me in the eyes and asked if I had anything I wanted to ask him. Without hesitation, I said no. It's not that I didn't have any questions; I had a million questions. But after having meditated quite intensively for over twenty years, having read over a hundred books on meditation and spiritually, and after having spent countless hours of contemplation on the subject, I knew that words could never adequately express any questions I had. Even more so, I knew that even if I could verbally formulate a question, such as: "Who Am I?" or "What is the ultimate reality of the universe, God, and myself?" these questions would still be just limited intellectual concepts that Guruji could never give an answer to. No one could give me an answer, as what I was interested in knowing had nothing to do with words or concepts, or even experience for that matter. What I was looking for could only be revealed from within.

Guruji had meetings all the next day. When he was finished, we all piled into our Suburban (me, Niki, the four kids, and Guruji) and drove to Philadelphia for Guruji's talk, which was at the Friends Meeting House in Center City. During the talk, Dylan lay down on a pew, fell asleep, and began to snore loudly. I started to go over so I could pick him up and carry him out of the room. Guruji saw me, and gestured to me to let him be. This made a big impression on me. Guruji was here to give a talk to an eagerly awaiting audience, but his concern was to not disturb a sleeping child.

CHAPTER 16

Advanced Course

In addition to the basic course (The Happiness Program), or Part 1 Course, which taught the Sudarshan Kriya, the Art of Living also offered an advanced course, or Part 2 Course, which was a meditation course. I was having really good experiences with the Sudarshan Kriya, and I wanted to take an advanced course, believing it might be beneficial in moving me forward on my spiritual path to enlightenment. In March of 1997 I attended a four-day Art of Living advanced course. It was held at the Burning Bush in Pittsburgh, which was an 1800s-era Roman Catholic convent now being used as a retreat center. The place had a great feel to it, old and dark, with very little updating.

This course focused on intensive, guided meditation and silence. Guided meditations are just that: Meditations where you are verbally guided as to where to put your attention. It was intensive in that we did a lot of meditation, maybe five or six hours per day. And silence meant that participants did not talk at all during the course. The instructor spoke and he led the course and told us what to do—when classes were, when meals were, when to go to bed—everything we needed to know. If we needed anything, or had any questions, we were advised to write it down on a piece of paper and give it to the instructor. The purpose of being silent was to get rid of one more thing that takes your awareness outward. Just as closing your eyes when you meditate helps to *bring* your awareness and attention inward, staying silent after you have finished meditating helps to *keep* your awareness and attention inward. Basically it made the whole course one big, continuous meditation. The combination of the many powerful guided meditations, along with continuous silence, had a profound effect. With each meditation, I went deeper and deeper into the transcendence, and when we weren't meditating, I remained in that silent space. I also did my own meditation practice for about two hours every day in my room. I was experiencing a new sense of what an ongoing, higher state of consciousness was all about. When the course was over, we were all brought out of silence and given the opportunity to share our experiences. It seemed that everyone felt the same heartfelt gratitude.

Unlike the Art of Living Part 1 Course, where you learn the Sudarshan Kriya and practice it every day, the guided meditations of the Part 2 Course are only done on the Part 2 Course; you don't practice them on your own. If you are so inclined, you may take the Part 2 Course as many times as you like. I really enjoyed the Part 2 Course and thought it would be very beneficial for my spiritual advancement, so I took two Part 2 Courses every year for more than fifteen years. Most of these courses I took at the Canadian International Art of Living Centre, which was a 250-acre retreat center located about halfway between Montreal and Quebec City. Part 2 silence courses are offered in different lengths, from three to ten days, and whenever possible I took ten-day courses.

CHAPTER 17

First Trip to India

In February of 2006 the Art of Living held their 25th anniversary silver jubilee celebration in Bangalore, India. I had always wanted to go to India, so I booked a two-week trip to join in the celebrations. The event was held at a 265-acre airfield and required over a dozen giant outdoor, movie-like screens so everyone could see. The main stage held 5,000 people in front of an audience of 2.5 million.

While in India, I learned that after the two weeks of celebrations and events, the Art of Living was going to offer the Blessings Course in Rishikesh, a small town in the Himalayan foothills that sits beside the Ganges River. It's the same town where Maharishi Mahesh Yogi had his famous ashram where the Beatles, Mia Farrow, Donovan, and others hung out in the late '60s, and the town is known as the Yoga Capital of the World. This was definitely a place I wanted to check out.

I delayed my flight by a week and booked a room in Rishikesh. I did not take the Blessings Course, because I wanted to explore the area. Every place I had visited in

India had felt crazy and high-energy, but Rishikesh was different. A relatively small city by Indian standards, with only about 100,000 people, Rishikesh was funky and laid-back. My room was on the second floor of the hotel, and had bars on the windows. I thought this was strange, as it would be hard for someone to reach these windows, and I asked the manager about it. He said the bars weren't to keep people out; they were to keep the monkeys out, so that they wouldn't steal people's stuff.

On my first full day, I went to Maharishi Mahesh Yogi's former ashram, which was just a short fifteen or twenty-minute walk from my hotel. The ashram, a four-teen-acre facility on the east bank of the Ganges River that Maharishi had built back in 1963, had long been abandoned. A high brick wall surrounded its perimeter, and the main entrance gate was protected by a guard. There were just a few of us tourists milling around when a local guy came by and said that for a few dollars each he could get us inside. We all gave him some money, and he called the guard over. They spoke for a moment, and our guide-to-be slipped the guard a handful of our money. The guard opened the gate and let us all in.

The ashram was overgrown and there was graffiti—mostly related to the Beatles and their 1968 stay—on the outsides and insides of its many buildings. The perimeter wall had been partially knocked down in several locations by, we were told, wild elephants. The place was deserted except for monkeys, who seemed to have taken over.

We toured the whole place—the large lecture halls where Maharishi used to gather with his followers and famous guests, the dormitory buildings, and the house where Maharishi lived when he stayed at the ashram.

Dozens of individual meditation huts squatted in a jungle-like area of the grounds. These small, egg-shaped buildings look like large beehives. They were spartan, two-story structures constructed of concrete and stones taken from the Ganges. Each had a first-floor living area of about ten feet by twelve feet with concrete stairs leading upstairs to a domed-ceilinged meditation space. Instead of the dormitories, people staying at the ashram could live in seclusion in these little huts, sometimes meditating for weeks on end. It appeared to me that Maharishi had meant for these individual stone cottages to be manmade meditation caves. In 1968, Mia Farrow's sister, Prudence, along with Mia and the Beatles, was on a retreat with Maharishi at the ashram. Prudence was very much into meditation, and she was spending all of her time meditating in one of the beehive huts. The Beatles had become concerned that Prudence was becoming a recluse, and they wanted her to come out to join the rest of the group. Out of this came Lennon's "Dear Prudence," which appeared on the *White Album*.

After about an hour of exploring, I left the ashram, strolling toward town with a stop at the Ganges River along the way. Since the earliest of times, the Ganges River (also known as the Ganga) has been revered as one of the most sacred rivers in the world. To Hindus, it *is* the most sacred. Hindus from all over India make an annual pilgrimage to the many temples and shrines located along its banks, believing it is auspicious to bathe, drink, and, after death, have their ashes scattered in this holiest of rivers. When I got to the Ganges, I came upon a sadhu who was bathing at the edge of the river. Sadhus are wandering ascetic holy men, or monks. Most are yogis who spend their lives in meditation and contemplation, seeking enlightenment. This sadhu wore only a loincloth and had long, unkempt dreadlocks. Besides a wooden staff, all he had with him was in a small cloth bag. Even though our lives were worlds apart, I felt a connection to this man: Just two guys trying to figure it all out.

I kept thinking about Maharishi's ashram, and how great it would have been to be there with him and the Beatles back in the '60s. The beehive meditation huts really intrigued me, and I definitely wanted to meditate in one. After lunch, I walked around town a bit and then went back to my hotel room. I decided that I would do my afternoon meditation at the ashram in one of the beehives. I grabbed a couple of pillows and the backrest I traveled with. As I was leaving the hotel, I told my manager friend what my plans were. He said, "Be careful," as there really were wild elephants that lived in the area, and they were known to sometimes hang out around the ashram.

I was pretty sure that the guard would not let me back in, so when I got there I walked around to a section of the perimeter wall that had been partially knocked down by elephants and was out of his sight. I climbed over and walked across the grounds toward the meditation huts. It was a little scary because the only living creatures were me and hundreds of monkeys. They clung to vines, trees, and portions of the buildings. Monkeys of all sizes, some missing feet or arms, and others swinging with infants clinging to their chests, chattered and collected around me. Our guide told us that morning that the monkeys were vicious, and the missing limbs were a result of the monkeys attacking one another.

I was relieved to reach the huts, and slipped into one. Though structurally sound, it was filthy from years of abandonment and neglect. I kept looking until I found one clean enough to occupy. I climbed the concrete stairs, entered the domed meditation area, and put down my backrest and pillows. Ultimately, while it was really cool to meditate in such an auspicious place, my meditation wasn't any different from those at home in my own bedroom.

As I walked back to my hotel, grateful to be unscathed by vicious monkeys or wild elephants, I remembered hearing Maharishi say in a teacher training video that the place where you meditate is not that important. He said it's best to have a private, clean, quiet place, but it is not a necessity. Maharishi had made another statement that I particularly needed to hear. He said that there was no need to go into the wilderness to find a cave to live and meditate in: Your room is your cave. Having heard this, my desire to live in a cave and meditate until I reached my so-called "enlightenment" had long left me.

The next day I went back to the ashram for my morning and afternoon meditations in the beehive hut, dropping off my meditation gear (backrest and pillows) afterwards, before walking around town to get something to eat and explore. The following day I again left my hotel to do my afternoon meditation program at the ashram. As always, I told my front-desk friend where I was off to. On my way back to the hotel, I walked by the Ganges, as was my normal route, and saw what appeared to be about 100 people next to, and actually in, the river a couple of hundred yards back. I walked over to see what was going on and saw that it was Guruji, Sri Sri Ravi Shankar, and the participants of the Blessing Course. They were doing the traditional dunking in the Ganges River, with many in the river getting wet, while others sat on the bank. I watched until it started to get dark, then left to get dinner. It was late, so I went straight to dinner instead of dropping off my things at the hotel first.

When I arrived back at the hotel, I found my friend pacing and upset. When I hadn't shown up at the hotel to drop off my stuff before dinner, he thought that I had been killed by a wild elephant. We talked for a while and I shared my desire to meditate in a cave. He knew just the place, and we made plans to go the next day on his motorcycle.

The next day, with my friend waiting outside, I stepped into the cave. I had to duck my head, as the ceiling was low. As my eyes adjusted to the darkness, I saw that it was a narrow space that extended back about fifty feet. My friend had told me that the cave had been occupied by various yogis over the years, but had been vacant for quite a long time. I slowly groped my way to the dark, dank back of the cave. Against the back wall, I discovered a seat carved out of stone. I sat in it and did an approximate thirty-minute meditation. Like at my beehive hut at Maharishi's ashram, I had a nice meditation, but it wasn't any different from my daily meditations at home.

Riding back, I thought how great it would be to go exploring on a motorcycle. I leaned forward and asked my friend if he knew of any place where I could rent one. He asked me if I knew how to ride a motorcycle, and I told him definitely. I had ridden motorcycles since I was a kid, and had owned three 650 Triumphs and currently owned a Harley.

He pulled over and got off, and said, "You drive." I slid forward, he got on behind me, and I drove us back to town. When we got to the hotel he said if I wanted, I could rent his motorcycle for seven dollars a day.

Driving in India, especially on a motorcycle, should have given me pause. Indian drivers were crazy. When I had first arrived in India a couple of weeks before, two of my friends and I took a taxi from the Bangalore Art of Living Ashram to Mysore, a 147-km drive. On a new, divided highway with two lanes going in each direction, we encountered two giant tour buses, one in each lane, coming straight toward us—on our side of the road. Our driver calmly pulled over to let them pass and then continued driving as if nothing had happened. When I asked why the buses were on our side of the road, he said, "Because there's less traffic on this side." The reason I could drive around Rishikesh was that where I was going, crazy driving was not an option.

The next morning I rode the motorcycle into the Himalayas. Paved roads yielded to gravel as soon as I left town. The roads, sometimes barely wide enough for even one car, hugged the mountains. I eased around hairpin turns with the mountain on one side and, in some spots, 1,000-foot drops on the other. The few other drivers on the road went slowly, sometimes backing up to let other vehicles pass. At one curve, there was a wide shoulder on the side of the road with a basin and hand-pumped well.

A young man pumped water for his small herd of cows and goats. I felt like I was in a *National Geographic* movie. I stopped at another section of the road that was especially scenic. I looked out for miles, observing crops growing on stepped mountainsides, with magnificent houses dotting the landscape, thinking how I wished every person I had ever known was there to see what I was seeing.

As I rode farther into the Himalayas, I was surprised to see that many of the people walking on the road looked much different from the others in India. They had what appeared to be Tibetan or Mongolian features. From the expressions I received as I rode by, they seemed to be just as surprised to see the likes of me. As I continued to ride, I saw a small village on the side of a mountain. I turned off the road and drove to the town. As I approached, I could see people milling around and what appeared to be some type of festivities. I came to some street vendors who were selling food on what was now no more than a dirt trail. One of them could speak a little English, and he told me that he would watch my bike for me while I went into the village. I parked next to his cart and walked on.

It was a little walled city that had no roads; just narrow dirt alleyways only about four or five feet wide and packed with people.

I smelled incense, heard chanting, and stopped walking. Peering through an open door, I saw a room crowded with people and flowers. A Hindu priest at the room's front was performing a spiritual ritual called a puja. I felt quite at home as I chose a spot on the dirt floor near the front to sit down. No one seemed to mind my presence, and I stayed for a while before continuing on.

I tipped the motorcycle-guarding vendor 100 rupees, and from his reaction it could have been a million dollars. We both smiled widely as I threw my leg over the bike and rode back to the hotel.

The next day I took a different route. I again headed north, into the Himalayas, but this time I road on the west side of the Chandrabhaga, a river that flows into the Ganges at Rishikesh. The journey brought me to a magnificent suspension footbridge spanning the river. I got off my bike and walked across the bridge, where I found a cave on the mountainside that overlooked the river. This natural cave was once home to some ancient yogi, as evidenced by plaques inside the small, one-person hollow. I didn't meditate in this spot, as it wasn't very private and did not have much attraction for me.

I continued on my ride, stopping at a little restaurant/general store to get some lunch. I think you know you are really getting off the beaten path when you're the only vehicle in a rocky parking area parked next to a couple of horses. After lunch, I continued on my one-person expedition before heading back to Rishikesh for my afternoon meditation in my beehive at the ashram. I spent one more day hanging out in Rishikesh, then took a taxi to Delhi for my flight home to the States.

CHAPTER 18

It Happened

After spending three weeks in India, I was back to my regular daily routine: Niki and the kids, work, T'ai Chi, qigong, yoga, and two hours of meditation. I also continued to take T'ai Chi and qigong classes, and went away for two or three weeks a year for intensive silent meditation courses. India was great, but I had all that I needed at home, as my path wasn't anywhere but where I was. I still wanted to do the Art of Living Blessings Course that I had elected to skip in India, and in May of 2007 I took the course at the Swami Dayananda ashram located on fourteen acres in the Pocono Mountains in Saylorsburg, Pennsylvania. As coincidence would have it, the Blessings Course in Rishikesh was also held at one of Swami Dayananda's ashrams.

The five-day Blessings Course was one in which participants learned to be a conduit to pass blessings on to others. I really had no interest in the stated purpose of the course of blessing other people; I just wanted to gather as much knowledge and experience as I could on my search for enlightenment. There were a little over 100 people on the course, and we were all doing various meditations and processes, when, on the fourth day, it happened.

We had just finished a meditation and were lying on the floor, on our backs with our eyes closed. I was in a really deep, deep state, and it felt like I was just floating in space. The course facilitators were walking around the room talking softly to each of the participants. Someone came over and very quietly asked me a few questions, and I responded. They then moved on to the next person. Immediately I felt this ball of energy, about the size of a grapefruit, hit me in the chest and enter my body. It was as if I had been struck by a blast from a very powerful air gun. My thought was that Guruji had somehow entered into me as this ball of energy. But how was this possible? He didn't even know I was on this course. I could not comprehend what had happened. Then straightaway I was hit in the chest by another ball of energy.

This second ball of energy was much larger than the first, about the size of a large medicine ball, and it wasn't like getting hit by a blast of air; it felt more like a meteor had just slammed into my chest. My immediate thought was that Christ, Krishna, and Buddha had all just entered me as this huge mass of energy. For whatever reason, this thought did not come to me as a belief; it came as a fact. This heavy mass of energy pinned me to the floor, and I was immobilized. It felt like I had an elephant sitting on my chest. Then, without warning, my chest arched up as my back came off the floor. My head tilted back, my mouth opened, and I expelled this grainy mass of small particles. This action, with this stuff coming out of my mouth, was like the scenes in the 1999 film *The Green Mile*, where Michael Clarke Duncan's character expels bad energy he took in. My upper body dropped back onto the floor, then again violently arched up as I expelled more of this "something" from my mouth. This action happened several more times before stopping as my body fell for the last time onto the floor.

I lay there with my eyes closed, feeling wiped out. I swam in an ocean of consciousness, or awareness, that was not separate from me; it was this oneness of consciousness/awareness/me. After a few minutes the entire class was instructed to come to a seated position, keeping our eyes closed. I sat up. We were then told to open our eyes. I opened my eyes.

Now I don't know how many times I had opened my eyes before, maybe a million, but I had never opened my eyes to anything like this in my fifty-seven years of occupying this body. The first thing I saw was a wall about forty feet in front of me with a large window in it. I couldn't see anything outside the window, as I really didn't see the window. All I saw was energy moving up and down and side to side. I knew I was looking at a window, but what I was seeing was energy, the essence of the window. A window that was not an inanimate object, but rather something that was full of vibrating, pulsating life. As I looked around the room, everything I saw was in the form of energy. The people in the room were all vibrating energy—energy that I could see as clear as day.

This energy had an undifferentiated sense of consciousness to it, and everything was this consciousness, my consciousness—an all-pervading, monolithic awareness. I knew immediately what had happened to me. I was enlightened. Class was dismissed and I went outside to sit on a bench that I found under a tree. Just sitting there, alone on that bench, I had the happiest, greatest, most overwhelming, all-pervading feeling of joy I had ever had. I vacillated between crying and laughing. Something that I had been looking for my entire life, I now had. Things I had read about, had hoped for, and had a vague understanding of, I was now living.

The Ultimate Reality does not come and go; it is always there. It is only our awareness of it that comes and goes. It was there before the manifest universe came into its apparent existence, and it will be there when this universe goes out of existence. If there were ever a time when it didn't exist, it wouldn't be the Ultimate Reality. That being said, I had not been enlightened an hour before, but now I was. How did I reconcile this? It's a little confusing. This feeling of "one-ness" that I experienced was a feeling that had always been there, something I had always felt. It was not a new feeling that was happening to me for the first time, even though I had never experienced it before. How can I explain this? I can't. Let me try, though, like this:

Imagine that you have always wanted to live in France, always wanted to go there, then one day someone tells you that you are in France and that you have always been in France. So now you know you're in France, but you don't feel any different than you felt before, but you're in France and you know it and you love it. Enlightenment is very subtle and totally overwhelming at the same time. There is an absolute sense of peace and tranquility, accompanied by unbounded, perfect joy. My experience was a totally new feeling that felt like something I had always felt. Something just barely under the surface of everything I had ever experienced, both internally and externally. It was like I suddenly became cognizant of this wonderful new feeling, this new awareness, and when I did, there was a sense that this was not a new awareness at all, but rather one that had always been there, only it was so subtle, so faint, that my attention hadn't picked up on it. I didn't become enlightened; I just *was* enlightened. It wasn't that my body and mind were now experiencing a new awareness, but rather it was that I now WAS this awareness, this awareness that encompassed everything and everyone, including the body and mind that I had been previously experiencing as me.

While I very quickly stopped seeing everything as vibrating energy, my experience of unbounded consciousness, with its attributeless attributes of happiness, contentment, and tranquil well-being was constant and never-changing—ever! When I left my bench and went to have lunch in the ashram cafeteria, nothing changed. As I ate, my expanded, all-pervading consciousness never left me. This was not the witnessing that I had been going in and out of for years. This was much more encompassing. Nothing I did diminished this state in any way. Nothing shook me out of this joyful bliss. I went back for my afternoon session, and something very strange was happening. As the course leader spoke to us, I knew what he was going to say, verbatim, before he spoke. I didn't tell anyone what was going on, but I think a few of my classmates knew something was happening.

After my afternoon session, I went back to my room to meditate. Nothing happened. Meditation always calmed my system and took me to a deeper, underlying state of transcendental consciousness, but now there was nowhere to go—I was already there. Dinner; evening session—no changes. Back to my room, I took a shower and went to sleep—no changes. I was sound asleep and there was no change in my state of consciousness. I was sleeping but my consciousness, my awareness, was awake. My body and mind were asleep, but I was no longer my body and mind. I was this consciousness, this awareness, which had a body and mind to function through, and this consciousness did not sleep. It experienced no changes, and again (and this is hard to explain) this new consciousness was more than an experience; it was me. It was not my mind, but my mind (and body) were an undivided part of it, and although it was definitely a new experience, my awareness of it was that it was not new at all. It had always been there, but somehow my attention had not picked up on it until it came to the overpowering forefront of everything.

The next morning I woke up—so to speak—meditated, and walked to the building where we were having our course. I met up with a friend whom I had known for years through the Art of Living. He told me that he was having a lot of back problems, with accompanying pain, and that he almost hadn't come to the course as his back was so bad, but for some reason he decided to come. I told him I had been doing qigong for years, and that I would be happy to do a qigong therapy treatment on his back, which may make it feel better.

The qigong I do is medical qigong. The practice is meant to keep you healthy. The exercises circulate the qi (prana) throughout your body, with certain exercises bringing in qi from the earth and the heavens (universe) and mixing it and circulating it with the qi in the body. The practice can also be used to treat others, using various techniques learned in our applied qigong therapy class. In recent years I have stopped treating people, but when I first started, I did it often. I remember one time I asked my son Dylan to let me practice on him. He was about seven years old. I gave him a complete, whole-body treatment, which took about fifteen to twenty minutes. When I was done I asked him how it was, and he said, "Great." I then asked him what he felt, and he said, "Nothing." The next night, Dylan was at the front door waiting for me when I came home. He asked if I would give him another qigong treatment. I took him upstairs and gave him a treatment and when I was done I asked him how it was, and again he said, "Great." I asked what he felt, and, like the night before, he said, "Nothing."

I said, "Dylan, how can it be great if you don't feel anything? You must feel something." He said he did feel something. I asked, "What?"

He thought for a few moments and then said, "I feel insects crawling all over my body, under my skin." What he was feeling was the qi moving through his body. He didn't know what it was, but he liked it.

I had my friend lie on the floor and I gave him a treatment. Treatments consist of both touching the person with your fingertips and palms, and also moving your hands over them without touching. This was like no treatment I had ever given before, as I was not giving the treatment, because I really was not there. I was just this mass of energy, this consciousness that was moving qi that was both a part of me and something separate, through my friend, who was also both a part of me and something separate. As much as I was feeling, my friend was also feeling, as he seemed to also be somewhat overwhelmed by the experience. Later that day he came over to me and told me that he now knew why he had come to the Blessings Course: It was so that he could get the qigong treatment I had given him.

We had some free time after our morning session, so I went to this huge flea market that was across the road from the ashram. This was a permanent market that happened on weekends, with stalls and booths for food sales, and tables for merchandise. The grounds were packed with both vendors and shoppers. What a trip this was! Talking to vendors was very strange. It wasn't me, this body talking; it was me, this expanded consciousness, speaking *through* this body, which I had previously taken to be me, and still *was* me, although it was more like just an accoutrement to this wonderful awareness. It took a bit of effort on my part to keep a straight face and not burst out laughing. What I really remember about walking through this mass of people was my take on what was going on as I watched these various folks moving around: Everything was perfect.

When I encounter people, I can be a little judgmental. I will often have an internal running dialogue of comments, like when I see extremely overweight people eating junk food, anyone drinking any kind of diet soda, and smokers. Don't people ever read the paper or watch the news? Anyhow, as I was walking around the flea market, every *thing* and every *one* was absolutely perfect in every way. All my internal comments stopped, and all I saw was perfection. I was just blissed out and nothing I saw or heard took me out of my bliss. In fact, everything seemed to add to it, if that was even possible. I'd walk by people smoking cigarettes and not only was there no condemnation going on in the back of my mind; there was just a joyous wonder to see them. Everything and everyone was, on one level, an undifferentiated part of this expanded consciousness, and everything was taking place just as it should, in a most natural and wonderful way. I'd see young, very overweight kids, who undoubtedly were being fed the same unhealthy diet as their accompanying overweight parents, shoveling in funnel cakes, while at the same time complaining to their parents who were scolding them, and it was like watching a fantastic movie taking place in a wonderland of perfection. Everything was just great. My mind was very much aware that it was processing everything that was coming in through the senses in a new way. It was not judging or commenting on anything. There was no good or bad. My mind was just allowing everything to be as it was, with nothing added. Everything was a movement of consciousness taking place in a vastness of awareness.

That afternoon the course ended and I drove back home to Haddonfield. Over the coming days, two things started to happen: The newness of this state I was in started to wear off, and my "enlightenment" consciousness started to fade. It was a very gradual process, but after about two weeks I was back to my "pre-enlightenment" consciousness. Now I have no complaints about my "normal" state of being, the state I was in prior to my awakening, but it is night and day when compared to the way I was during my brief period of "enlightenment." My mind was back to its old habits of putting labels on and categorizing things; not everything, but a lot of stuff.

So when I *became* enlightened, why did I have the contradictory sense that while this feeling was a new one for me, it was at the same time a feeling that I had always felt? It was because while I had not been *knowingly* experiencing this state before, I had been *subconsciously* experiencing it all along. The Self does not come and go. It is always there. And while we do have an ongoing awareness of it during our normal waking state, this awareness is not a *conscious* one, as our awareness of it is so fleeting that it passes unnoticed by our minds.

We have all heard of subliminal advertising. This is where advertisers put out messages that are below the threshold of perception of the conscious mind, yet are picked up unconsciously by the subconscious mind. Audio messages may be played at very low volume, or visual images flashed so quickly that consciously there is no awareness of this messaging. This messaging has, however, been unknowingly recorded somewhere deep inside.

The Absolute, the Self, is the screen upon which the apparent manifest universe is projected. It is also the medium that supports our own individual awareness. We are not consciously aware of this screen of the Absolute, as it is obscured by a veil of unending thoughts: Our musing of past events, our thoughts of the present condition we are experiencing, and our concerns and anticipations of things to come. Yet in between all these passing thoughts is an instant between one train of thought and the next that is thought-free. In this infinitesimally brief moment, which is also present at the point of transition between the waking and sleep states, the Absolute is unmasked. This revelation of the Self is so fleeting, however, that the conscious mind is unable to pick up on it and it goes by unnoticed. It is experienced by all; just not consciously. What happened to me was that there was an instantaneous *shift* in my consciousness where the silent, pure consciousness of the Self became the predominate state of my mind, and my once-predominating thoughts were now what was fleeting. My mind had a silent, still awareness of all that it was experiencing, with none of its customary participations taking place. This ever-existent awareness of the Self included my heretofore unconscious awareness of it, thus the sense that this "new" experience that was taking place was one that I had always felt.

Thinking back on my course, I found it so strange that this ball of energy, which I took to be Guruji, hit me in the chest. Guruji had no idea that I was even on that course. And what was it that actually hit me? The only way I can describe it is as a *ball of energy* that had some type of mass to it. And as to that second ball of energy? I have no idea what that was about or why I immediately had the incontrovertible belief that it was Christ, Krishna, and Buddha entering into me.

There are a lot of stories floating around from followers of Guruji about some really unexplainable stuff that he has supposedly done. Marcy Jackson, a longtime devotee of Guruji and a friend of mine, in her book *Tales Beyond The Known* talks about many of the crazy things she has witnessed and experienced over the years while being around, and traveling with, Guruji. Some of this stuff is just unbelievable. Thinking of my experience reminded me of something that happened several years before, while attending a course at the Art of Living's Canadian ashram. It was summertime and there were several hundred people on the course. A huge tent with a wooden floor had been erected to accommodate everyone. During these large courses, there is a stage for Guruji and next to it is a spot for people to play music and lead everyone in bhajans (Hindu devotional songs). Sometimes people get up and dance.

At these events, most people sit on the floor, but there are chairs in the back of the room for those who prefer to sit in a chair. There was a row of chairs in the back of the tent, and I was sitting on one of the chairs. During one of the bhajans, a young woman, who was about thirty feet in front of me, got up and started to dance. The whole room was facing the stage, and this person had no idea that I was behind her and watching her dance. Shortly after this woman started to dance, another woman, who was about ten feet in front of me, got up and also started to dance, blocking my view of the woman I had been watching. My thought was: *I wish this woman who just got up would sit down so I can keep watching the first woman dance.* I knew this was never going to happen, as once someone gets up to dance, they invariably stay standing and keep dancing until the song is over. With that, the woman dancing in the front, whom I could no longer see, moved several feet to the side and then turned and walked toward the back of the tent. When she got to the row of chairs where I was sitting, a row that was only a couple of feet behind the people sitting on the floor, she turned and made her way down the row, until she was standing directly in front of me. She then turned toward the stage and continued dancing! Now when I say this woman was dancing right in front of me, I mean *right* in front of me. I mean, I literally had to move my feet to give her room to dance. How was this even possible? There was no logic to what had just happened. My only thought was: *Guruji, you rascal*! When the song was over, the woman made her way back to where she had been sitting and sat down.

CHAPTER 19

Hiking the Himalayas

Meditating in a cave in India scratched that one off my bucket list, but I still had one more item—hiking through the Himalayas. Ever since I had started reading about enlightenment and the spiritual journey, I had wanted to hike through the Himalayas. I thought Nepal would be the place to go, but when I started doing more in-depth research, I decided that Bhutan would be a much better place. Nepal received a lot of travelers and the hiking trails were not all that pristine. Bhutan, on the other hand, was in a much more natural state. Bhutan is located above the northeastern section of India and borders Tibet. Nepal's population was about 25 million people, whereas Bhutan, with one-third the landmass, had only 600,000. Bhutan is a benevolent Buddhist kingdom that hasn't changed much in the last 1,000 years. The country got its first TVs in 1999, and it is the place where they aren't as much concerned with Gross National Product as they are with Gross National Happiness. There was never going to be a good time to go as far as money, time, and work were concerned, so I decided to just do it and I booked a trip for the fall of 2007.

Bhutan is a little more difficult to get into and travel through, compared to most countries. Visitors are not allowed anywhere without a Bhutanese guide, and are required to obtain visas through registered tour operators before even entering the country. The trek I wanted to take was to Chomolhari, a 24,035-foot mountain that straddles Tibet and Bhutan, and is considered sacred by both Tibetan and Bhutanese Buddhists. The fifteen-day trip, which included trekking eighty-five miles at elevations as high as 17,200 feet, was described by the trekking company as a challenging and strenuous trek, appropriate only for experienced hikers. Some days demanded up to fourteen miles of hiking. Conditions would be so harsh that participants were required to submit applications and be accepted onto the tour. At fifty-seven years old, I had never done anything like this before. My application was denied. I did not have the necessary experience, and the tour company felt that the trip would be too difficult for me. I put my lawyerly skills of persuasion to work and explained that even though I had never done anything as intense as this before, I was in great shape and could do it no problem. I was still told no go, but after several more persistent phone calls on my part, I talked my way onto the trip.

I had five months to get ready. Having no idea how hard the trip would be, I wanted to be sure that I actually *was* in good enough shape to do it. I bought a pair of hiking boots and started to break them in and get into hiking shape. Our supplies were going to be carried by packhorses, so all I had to carry was a daypack with rain gear, extra clothes for warmth, water, and a water purifier. I bought a really good daypack, loaded it with everything I would have to carry, and started walking. I walked seven miles a day, several days a week. After a few months, I added walking up and down two flights of stairs several days a week, going up and down two stairs at a time with my pack on for an hour straight. I walked in all kinds of weather, from beautiful sunny days to pouring rain. I also increased my running, going from my normal three miles, three days per week, to seven miles, three days per week. Toward the very end, I increased my running to five days per week, and two days before the start of my trip, I tore something in my knee during my seven-mile run. I'm not sure what I did to my knee, but it hurt badly and I could barely walk. I hoped it would get better overnight, but the next day, the day before my departure, it was just as bad, if not worse. I called a friend, who was an orthopedic surgeon, and told him of my dilemma. He came over and checked my knee, which was severely swollen, and on my dining room floor he injected my knee with cortisone. My knee, though still injured, felt fine and the next day I boarded my flight for Bhutan.

The first leg of my trip was to Bangkok, Thailand, where I was to rendezvous with the tour company's American guide, Marin, and my fellow trekking travelers. I arrived in Bangkok in the early morning and spent the day exploring the city. That evening I met up with Marin. She informed me that there would only be two people on the trek—a woman from California and me. The next morning the three of us boarded our flight to Paro, the only city in Bhutan with an international airport. The airline that we were flying in on was Drukair, the Royal Bhutan Airline, the only airline that flew into Bhutan besides Bhutan Airlines. As we made our approach for landing, our pilot came on the intercom to tell us not to be alarmed, *but*, as Bhutan is so mountainous, they had to build the airport in the mountains, and we couldn't come in on a straight approach, as there were mountains at both ends of the runway. We would descend from the side, flying straight toward one of the mountains at the end of the runway and then, at the last minute, make a sharp turn to orient over the runway. It was a little hairy, but it made our entry into Bhutan that much more exciting.

At the airport we met our two Bhutanese guides, a man in his early thirties and another in his mid to late forties. These guides, along with Marin, would lead us on our trek and be with us for the entire trip. We cleared customs and went to our hotel to rest up, as the next day we were going to be touring the Paro Valley and hiking up to Taktsang, the Tiger's Nest Monastery, said to be the holiest site in all of Bhutan. Legend has it that 1,300 years ago, Guru Rinpoche, an Indian Buddhist monk, flew on the back of a flying tiger from Tibet to Taktsang and meditated in a cave there for three years before spreading Buddhism to Bhutan. Years later, a monastery, the Tiger's Nest, was built at the site of the cave, a sheer cliff 3,000 feet above the Paro Valley below. This first day's hike would take us up to over 10,000 feet.

The tour company had advised us to bring altitude sickness pills, as many people suffer in these extreme heights. I had brought pills, but I wasn't sure I wanted to take them, as I am averse to taking any kind of medication unless it's absolutely necessary. That first afternoon, on the day before our hike up to the Tiger's Nest Monastery, I was in my hotel room and in the middle of my meditation when I took this huge breath. I then became aware that I had stopped breathing, as I sometimes do during meditation, and then started again by leading off with a huge breath that filled my lungs to their full capacity. This was a yogic breath where my stomach extended as I filled my lower lungs and then came in a little as I filled my middle and upper lungs. I then let go totally as all the air was expelled. I realized that breathing like this would fill my lungs with a tremendous amount of air, much more than during normal breathing, and that if I breathed like this for my trip, I would most likely not get altitude sickness, as I would be getting more than enough oxygen, even at altitudes of over 17,000 feet. I decided that I would not take my altitude sickness pills and hoped for the best.

Our first stop that next morning was Kyichu Lhakhang Monastery. I told my Bhutanese guides that I was a longtime meditator and was really interested in seeing these holy places. This first monastery was so old that there were indentations in the thick wooden floors caused by monks kneeling to meditate over many, many centuries. After speaking to our Bhutanese guides, one of the monks at the monastery took me aside and led me to a quiet, secluded room where I could meditate. It was uplifting knowing that for over a 1,000 years Buddhist monks had meditated in this same room that I was in. That afternoon we went to the Tiger's Nest, hiking up 3,000 feet on a small trail that led to the monastery. This monastery, which consisted of a cluster of buildings and courtyards, was built on a cliff that overlooked the valley. We stopped on our hike up the mountain at a spot with a great vista to take some pictures. As I was walking over to a large rock where I could stand to take my pictures, one of our guides came over and told me to be careful, as someone recently had been standing on this same rock talking pictures when, without paying attention, they stepped back and fell off, falling straight down over 2,000 feet to their death. I was very careful.

Shortly after we arrived at the monastery, one of the monks came over and escorted us to a temple building located at the back of the compound. This building was locked and off limits to the public. The monk took out a very large key and opened what appeared to be an ancient lock and led me inside, shutting the door behind us. He handed me a blanket to sit on and told me that I could meditate in this very sacred temple within the monastery. He left me alone to meditate. I wasn't sure why I was singled out and allowed into this part of the monastery. I assumed it was because one of our guides had said something to the monks when we first arrived. I was alone in this secluded small temple room in the Tiger's Nest Monastery, situated on a cliff at a 10,000-foot elevation in the Himalaya Mountains, 3,000 feet above the Paro Valley below. I meditated for only about thirty minutes, as the other members of my party waited outside. If I were there alone, I would have stayed in that temple meditating for hours, even days if they would have let me. It wasn't that my meditation was any better there than my meditations at home in my room; it was just that this was a very auspicious place to be. I finished my meditation and came out of the temple to rejoin my group and resume our tour of the monastery.

The next day we started our trek through the Himalayas. Early in the morning, we drove to the edge of town to meet up with the rest of our support staff—two cooks and two horsemen. Ten horses would carry all the supplies we needed for the eleven day, eighty-five–mile trek—food, cooking equipment, clothing, tents, sleeping gear, tables, chairs—everything. Every day we would rise to have breakfast, and then start our hike. One of our Bhutanese guides would carry our lunch in a large backpack. Our cooks and horsemen would stay behind to break camp and load up the horses. At some point during the day, they would catch up to us and continue on ahead to set up camp at a predetermined location where we would meet up for dinner and the night.

The first night of our trek we camped next to a stream. The next day, after finishing my morning meditation in my tent, I put on a bathing suit, slipped on my sandals, and walked over to the cooking tent where all the Bhutanese staff slept. I asked to borrow a small pot that I could use to rinse off when I took a bath in the stream. Our head guide told me that I could not take a bath, as the water was too cold and I would get sick and die. I said, "No way, I'll be perfectly fine," and talked him into giving me a pot. I walked over to the stream and got in and took a morning bath. It was cold—real cold—but after I was done and dried off and got dressed, I felt great. There was no way I was going to go for eleven days without bathing. It ended up that each night we camped next to either a stream or a river, and each morning I took a bath. Some nights it snowed a little, and the next morning I'd walk over the snow in my sandals and bathing suit to get my pot from the cooks to take my bath. One night we had an ice storm and the tents were iced in with about an eighth of an inch of ice. I broke the ice off my tent so I could get out, and trudged across the ice to get my pot, then into the stream and the freezing water for my morning ritual. The entire staff, including Marin, told me that they had never had anyone ever get into the water on one of these treks, and I think the Bhutanese guides were truly amazed that I didn't drop dead from the cold.

On the third night of our trek, we set up at the base camp of Chomolhari, at an elevation of 13,250 feet. We remained there the next day to allow our bodies to acclimate to the elevation before going higher. There were quite a number of other tour groups that were camping with us at the base camp of Chomolhari. During that day of acclimatization, we were told that we could either hang out around base camp to rest up, or we could do a day hike in the area. I told my Bhutanese guides that I would like to hike up a nearby mountain. Marin and the woman on the trek with me said that they would like to hike up with us. About one-third of the way up the mountain, my fellow trekker decided to turn back, as it was too much for her. Marin had a knee that was bothering her, and she also needed to stay with the other trekker, so they hiked down together. The guides and I continued to the top of the mountain. The views were spectacular, with Chomolhari on the one side and base camp, far below, on the other. We took some time checking out the majesty of it all, and then the Bhutanese guides asked me what I wanted to do now. Next to us was a peak that went straight up, the entire side covered with rocks that had slid down due to its steepness. I jokingly said, "Let's climb that peak."

The guides said, "Okay," and they started to hike over to its base.

I said, "No, I was just kidding." I didn't think it would even be possible to climb, as it was so steep and rocky.

They said, "Okay, let's go down."

I then said, "Wait a minute, you guys actually want to climb that thing?"

They said, "No, we're just here to do what you want to do." It was obvious to me that they really did want to climb that peak.

I said, "If you guys want to climb it, let's go!" (I really didn't want to climb it, as it seemed a little scary, but if they thought it was possible, I was going to go with them.)

I had no idea how high the peak was, maybe another 300 feet above where we were. This was an absolutely incredible place to be—far above the tree line, with a 360-degree view of snow-covered mountains in every direction. We were all enjoying our accomplishment when the guides said that we needed to gather some rocks and make a monument. I asked why. They said that in Bhutan, when someone climbs a mountain peak for the first time, they erect a stone monument so future climbers will know that someone has climbed the peak before. They said there was no monument on this peak, which meant that we were the first to ever scale it. We made our monument and took our pictures next to it. The guides then told me that I had just climbed higher than anyone who had ever been on a trek with them before had climbed.

As my Bhutanese guides and I were usually well

ahead of Marin and my co-traveler, I was starting to feel pretty good about myself and what great shape I was in. After all, these guys were from Bhutan and they were used to these elevations, and I had no problem keeping up with them. That sense of being in such good shape soon vanished. The trails and paths that we used for our trek zigzagged as they went up and down the mountains, as everyone used these for travel and transportation, and walking straight up or straight down would be way too arduous, especially at these elevations. As we were hiking up one of the mountainside trails, we passed another group that was making their way down. This other group was the support staff for another tour and included their horses and gear. As they passed by, our guides told us to get to the uphill side of the trail, because sometimes the horses try to bump you as they go by, knocking you down the mountain. This other group was following the trail, zigzagging down the mountain, and they were about 100 yards downhill from us when our older guide, the guy in his mid- to late-forties, decided to go down to them to get something. He didn't walk back down the trail to reach the other group; he ran down the mountain—straight down. After he got what he went for, he ran back up to us—straight up. He moved like a gazelle. I realized that I was in nowhere near the shape that these guys were in, nor would I ever be.

As I walked with my guides all day long, we got to talk a lot. We talked about our countries, our families, the world—everything. Bhutan is a Buddhist kingdom, and in most families one of the sons becomes a Buddhist monk. My younger guide was not married and had no kids, but the older one was, and had a son who was in school to become a monk. He told me that Bhutan had Buddhist monasteries, but the boys who went to these monasteries usually just ended up officiating at weddings and funerals and things like that. His son wanted to receive a very high level of training, a training that he didn't think he could get in Bhutan, so his parents sent him to the *Namdroling* Monastery in Mysore, India. This renowned Tibetan Buddhist monastery was the largest teaching center of the Nyingma (ancient) lineage of Tibetan Buddhism in the world. I asked my guide how long the training was, and he said twenty years. I then asked how long his son had been there, and he said twelve years. I had been to Mysore and I knew it was quite a distance (1,750 miles), and I asked my guide how often he and his wife got to see their son. He told me that his son was able to come home one time during the first couple of years of his training, but he hadn't been back since, and he wouldn't be able to come home again until after he finished his remaining eight years of training. I asked him if he had any plans to go visit his son, and he said he got to talk to his son on the phone, and he sent him care packages, but he couldn't afford the trip to go see him.

This really bothered me. I've got four kids, and if one of them went off to school for twenty years and I couldn't go to see them and they could only come home one time to visit, I think I'd go crazy. The next day I asked him how much it would cost for him to go visit his son. He said he had looked into it and told me how much it would cost for the entire trip, including train fare, food, and lodging. I did the exchange rate and it worked out to almost three-hundred dollars. I then asked him if he were able to go, would his wife want to go with him, and he said yes. That next day I handed him six $100 bills. Needless to say, he was pretty taken aback. He couldn't believe it. He was so excited to tell his wife, but he had to wait, as we were still in the mountains and had no cell service. Of the Bhutanese staff, only the two guides spoke fluent English. I told the younger one, who was actually the head guide, that while I was planning on giving everyone a tip, it would be nowhere near the amount that I had just given his coworker. He completely understood, as did the rest of the staff, and there were no hard feelings. They were all just very happy for their friend.

Hiking through the Himalayas was all that I had hoped it would be. During the entire eighty-five–mile trek, we never saw a road or utility pole of any kind. All travel was done on the small paths or trails we used, and everything was carried over these paths and trails on the back of a person, a horse, or a yak. We never saw any man-made structures except for an occasional house or primitive hut used by the herders who raised yaks. We passed one house where the family was preparing for a bath. An old hollowed-out log, filled with water, sat solidly in the yard. A wood fire, partially buried in river rocks, blazed next to the log. The women were heating these rocks over the fire and were then going to drop them into the hollowed-out log to heat the water in the family bathtub.

Many times during my trek, I found myself alone with just my two Bhutanese guides, far ahead and out of sight of Marin and my co-traveler, looking out in all directions and seeing no one—no man-made structures; no trees; just vast expanses of snow-peaked mountains and valleys. This nature-induced sense of isolation brought on a feeling of expansion and connection, a oneness with my natural surroundings. It was easy to understand why the Himalayas were considered such sacred mountains.

We finished our trek and got loaded into a small van that was waiting to take us back to Paro and our hotel. It really felt great getting back to the lower Paro Valley elevation of 7,200 feet. Both Marin and my co-traveler suffered from bouts of altitude sickness during our trek (headaches and not feeling well). While I never got altitude sickness, I sometimes had a hard time sleeping at night, as it was difficult to get all the oxygen that my system wanted. It was nice to be back to a lower elevation and not be oxygen-deprived or have to even think about breathing.

CHAPTER 20

Nepal

Since I had to fly halfway around the world to get to Bhutan, I decided when I first booked my trip that I would add an extra week so that I could travel to Nepal; not for trekking, but just to spend time in Katmandu. Marin had friends in Katmandu she wanted to visit, and she accompanied me for my extended excursion. Katmandu had a funky, international vibe that at times felt like it was in a 1960s hippie time warp. The city was crowded, with people visiting from all over the world. Marin had been to Katmandu something like forty times, and she had the place wired. We went all over. She knew a guy who owned a music store who sold everything from Tibetan singing bowls to Indian tabla drums. We visited a friend of hers who was from Kashmir. He owned a rug store, selling only artisan Kashmirian rugs. They were exquisite. One of her friends was from Tibet and had a jewelry store where he made jewelry from stones he brought in from Tibet. This guy was extremely talented, and made some unbelievably gorgeous stuff. We also went to knife stores, hat stores, funky stores (Freak Street Namaste Beads House), and great restaurants (Mike's Breakfast). We saw it all.

We also visited a couple of temples. The first was Boudhanath Stupa; a Buddhist stupa located seven miles outside of downtown Katmandu. A stupa is a mound-like structure containing relics, typically the remains of Buddhist monks or nuns, and used as a place of meditation. This ancient stupa, one of the largest in the world, is the largest stupa in Nepal, and is considered the holiest Tibetan Buddhist temple outside of Tibet. In 1979, UNESCO named it a World Heritage Site.

We next went to Pushupatinath Temple, the oldest Hindu temple in Katmandu, dating back to at least 400 AD. This temple is regarded as the most sacred among the temples of Lord Shiva, the Hindu God of destruction. Hindus believe that the universe flows in a continuous circle with Brahma, the creator of the universe, Vishnu, the preserver of the universe, and Shiva, the destroyer of the universe, after which Brahma again creates the universe and so on. Hindus from all over Nepal and India come here for the last several weeks of their lives to meet death and then be cremated on open-air stone platforms that are situated along the sacred Bagmati River on which the temple sits. The Bagmati later meets the holy river Ganges. Hindus believe that if they die at the Pushupatinath Temple and are cremated and their ashes put into the Bagmati River, they will then be reborn as humans regardless of any misconduct during their lifetime. We saw a few open-air cremations in progress. The recently deceased were wrapped in colorful cloths and placed on pyres next to the river. Oil was then poured into their mouths and they were covered with loose straw and straw mats, and then set on fire. After everything had been consumed by fire, the ashes were swept into the river. Marin told me that in the past, she had seen some people who were a little too anxious to see their loved ones move on, for when the oil was poured into the mouths of the recently deceased, the very much alive corpses spat it out. Thankfully, we did not see any of that on this day.

We did see quite a few sadhus, wandering ascetic yogis, who were hanging around the temple grounds. These guys had very unique appearances; wearing everything from colorful robes to simple loincloths. All had their bodies painted in a multitude of colors. Some of the sadhus spoke English, and I went over to speak to a group of five of them. I asked them about their spiritual practices and meditations and who their gurus were. One of them told me how healthy he was and said he could drink water straight out of the Bagmati River without getting sick. This river was gross. In addition to all the ashes that were swept into it from the cremations, the water was muddy with trash floating everywhere, and people were bathing in it. It seemed to me that you could get some kind of weird disease by just touching this water. I told the sadhu that that was great, but I had no interest in seeing him drink from this river. I gave the sadhus some money, as was the custom, and Marin took a few pictures of me with them. One of my favorites is of me sitting in a full lotus position with one of the sadhus sitting next to me in nothing but a loincloth, with one of his legs in position for lotus and his other leg wrapped behind his shoulder and head.

After spending a little over three weeks in Thailand, Bhutan, and Nepal, I boarded my flight home to Niki and the kids, and got back into the groove of work. I did my two-hour-a-day meditation practice every day during my trip, but now that I was home, I once again became more regular with my daily T'ai Chi, qigong, and yoga practices. My trip to the Himalayas was all I had hoped it would be, but as far as my spiritual practices go, the place I'm in makes no difference, and it is always good just to be home.

CHAPTER 21

Second Trip to India

My daughter Maddie went to the University of Delaware for her undergraduate schooling, and for their winter break, in addition to having Christmas off, they had off the whole month of January. She wanted me to take her someplace "exotic" for her extended vacation, so I booked a trip for the two us to go to India for twenty-three days in 2010. We flew into Cochin, in the state of Kerala, and took a taxi to our hotel. Our driver was a maniac, as a lot of Indian drivers are, and Maddie was a little freaked out and had doubts we'd make it to our hotel in one piece, but we did. Having been to India before and having seen how people drive, I was a little less concerned, but still, it was a pretty insane ride, weaving in and out of traffic, and going way too fast for the conditions.

Cochin is on the Malabar Coast, along the Arabian Sea in southwest India. After a couple of days exploring the area, we met up with the driver I had hired to take us around Southern India: A fellow in his late twenties who had a nice, well-kept car, and was a very good driver. Our first stop was the Kerala backwaters; a labyrinth of waterways made up of rivers, canals, and lakes that extends for over 900 kilometers. Almost all of life in this area travels exclusively by this immense network of waterways. I had hired a houseboat with a crew of three to take us on a three-day excursion through these backwaters.

During our backwater adventures, we were somewhat surprised to find a large Christian presence in what seemed like the middle of nowhere and accessible only by water. We came upon and visited a Catholic school, a convent, and a very old beautiful Catholic church. It seems that St. Thomas, one of the original twelve disciples of Jesus, had arrived on the Kerala coast in 52 AD to preach the Gospel and baptize people, founding what is today known as the St. Thomas Christians.

Kerala has beautiful beaches, and after our boat trip ended, our driver was waiting to take us south to Varkala Beach on a road that hugged the coast. There was a set of rosary beads hanging from the rear-view mirror, and I asked our driver about it. He said he was a Muslim, but his boss, the owner of his car, was a Christian. I asked about the religious makeup of the area, and he said that there were mostly Hindus, Muslims, Christians, and Buddhists. I asked how they all got along, and he said everyone got along fine with no problems. I asked why he thought everyone got along so well, and he said it was due to education. He said that while education is supposedly mandatory for all of India, in the state of Kerala, all kids are actually made to go to school and that going to school together, and getting educated, helped give the kids a healthy respect for one another and their religions.

We spent a few days at Varkala Beach and then continued south to Kollam Beach. On the way, we stopped at a small fishing village just outside of Kollam that was the home of the ashram of Mata Amritanandamayi, known simply as Amma, or Mother. This ashram was hard to miss, as it was like a small city. It could accommodate several thousand visitors and residents, and all of the buildings were pink. Amma is known as the "hugging guru," as she greets all who come to see her (over 36 million people worldwide) with a long hug. Hoping to get a hug, we walked across a large bridge (which of course was pink) to get to the ashram, but when we got there, we found that a huge retreat had just ended and we had just missed her. We walked around for a while, and I bought Maddie some ice cream and picked up a couple of Amma's books for myself.

After spending a few days at Kollam Beach, we headed northeast for a two-day drive to Tiruvannamalai to visit the ashram of Sri Ramana Maharshi. As always, we stopped at every major Hindu temple we came to. One temple was near the extremely sacred city of Madurai, where we were to spend our first night. We had to walk up a fairly steep hill to get to this temple, and it was quite a hike, but when we got to the top and attempted to go in, we were told by the person at the entrance (who didn't speak much English) that we could not come in, as the temple was only open to Hindus. I'm not a follower of any particular religion, but I really wanted to see this temple, so I told the guy that we were Hindus. He looked at us and said: "No, not Hindus," and he was not going to let us in.

I may not be a Hindu, but I know an awful lot about Hinduism. I threw out the names of several of the more important works in Hinduism—*The Bhagavad Gita*, *The Mahabharata*, *Vasistha's Yoga*; followed by the names of some of the major Hindu deities—Vishnu, Shiva, Krishna; followed by my recital, in Sanskrit, of one of their more well-known mantras—*"Om Namo Bhagavate Vasudevaya"* (Om, I bow to Lord Vasudeva or Lord Krishna). This somewhat astonished guy then said: "Oh, Hindus!" and I nodded my head. I paid our entrance fees and we went in. The temple was ancient, and we could feel the spirituality and stillness as we checked out every nook and cranny, all the while receiving quite a few strange looks from the Hindus who were there and wondering how we got in.

We left the temple and walked back down the hill to our car and driver, and continued on to our hotel in Madurai. The next morning we left for the place I most wanted to see in all of India—Tiruvannamalai, the home of Sri Ramanasramam, the ashram of the late Sri Ramana Maharshi. I had wanted to visit Tiruvannamalai and Sri Ramana Maharshi's ashram on my first trip to India but hadn't had the time. I had learned of Sri Ramana Maharshi over ten years before when, while browsing through a New Age bookstore in Philadelphia, I came upon a book about his life and teachings. This guy was the real deal. To me, he was one of the greatest enlightened masters of all times. Born in 1879, he became spontaneously enlightened in 1896 at the age of sixteen. Drawn at an early age to Tiruvannamalai's holy mountain, Arunachala, he traveled there shortly after his enlightenment, living in or around Tiruvannamalai's various temples before moving to the holy mountain in 1899, where he stayed for the remainder of his life. Maharshi, or Sri Bhagavan as he was also known, spent his first seventeen years on Arunachala living in Virupaksha Cave, a small cave on the mountainside. He spent his next six years living in Skandashram Cave, which was higher up the mountain. In 1922, Sri Bhagavan moved to the base of the mountain so as to meet the needs of the many people who had come to Arunachala to seek him out; both for his spiritual instruction and, more importantly, just to be near him. An ashram was built up around him, where he lived until his death in 1950.

Sri Bhagavan spoke very little, usually not at all, from the time of his enlightenment in 1896 until he moved to the base of the mountain in 1922. Those who visited him during that time period would be received in silence. When Maharshi moved to the base of Arunachala in 1922, he started to speak so as to satisfy the desires of the many who came from all over the world to see him, but his preferred method of communication was always silence. Although Maharshi gave his approval to a variety of paths and methods of spiritual pursuit, his main recommendation was that of self-enquiry with the focus on the question of "Who am I?" One of the greatest things about Sri Ramana Maharshi's teachings is that during most of the years when he was speaking and answering the many questions of those who came to see him, all of the questions and answers were written down contemporaneously. These questions and answers have since been published in book form. So, unlike many of the teachings of the ancient masters, we actually know exactly what Maharshi said.

As we will discuss more in depth later, the Ultimate Truth cannot be comprehended on the level of the thinking mind, and, as such, cannot be put into words. Words used in trying to convey it, no matter how lofty, are really just mindless prattle creating only intellectual concepts in the mind of the listener. Sri Bhagavan didn't speak the Ultimate Truth—he *was* the Ultimate Truth—and it radiated from him. The stories are legendary regarding the many people who were so moved and transformed by Sri Bhagavan—not by his words—but by his silence, which penetrated deeply into all who were so fortunate as to be in his presence.

The first thing Maddie and I did after checking into our hotel room in Tiruvannamalai was to head straight to Arunachala and the Sri Ramanasramam. We walked through the main gates and found the place buzzing with activity. There were people there from all over the world, all of whom had come to be at the place where this spiritual giant had lived for so many years. After a quick survey of the buildings and grounds, we walked to the back of the ashram and through a small gate that led to a trail that went up the mountain. I wanted to find the caves where Sri Bhagavan had spent twenty-three years, mostly in silence, absorbed in samadhi, a state of deep spiritual awareness of the Self. We left our shoes at the edge of the trail, as we wanted to climb the mountain in the traditional way— barefoot. As we started up, we passed some local stonecutters who had set up to sell their wares to those going up the mountain. I wanted to get something, so we stopped and I purchased a small hand-carved stone Ganesha, the well-known elephant-headed Hindu deity widely revered as the remover of obstacles.

As we continued up the trail, we started to pass monkeys—lots of monkeys. These weren't the big, scary monkeys, like the ones I had encountered at Maharishi Mahesh Yogi's ashram in Rishikesh during my first trip to India. These were smaller monkeys that seemed very friendly and came right up to us. Maddie wanted to stop and play with every monkey she saw, and it was all I could do to keep her moving. We came to a clearing where we were able to see the town of Tiruvannamalai and the Annamalalyar Temple below. The Annamalalyar Temple is one of the largest temples in India, covering over twenty-four acres. It is also one of the tallest, with its tallest tower rising up 217 feet. This Hindu temple, built in the ninth century, was dedicated to the deity Shiva. It was a spectacular sight, and we had a passerby take our picture with the town and the temple below in the background.

As we continued up the mountain trail, the first cave we came to was Virupaksha where Sri Bhagavan had spent seventeen years. Maddie wasn't that interested in going into the cave, so I left her outside to play with the monkeys while I went in. This stone cave was really small, barely large enough for four people. There were a couple of people already in the cave, but I managed to squeeze into a little spot by a wall and sit down to meditate. It was really satisfying to be able to meditate in the cave where Sri Bhagavan had spent so many years. I wasn't trying to attain any spiritual revelations or feel his presence; I just wanted to be there. After a short meditation, I left the cave and pulled Maddie away from her monkeys as we continued up the mountain.

The trail got narrower and steeper as we eventually made our way to the Skandashram Cave. Maddie again wanted to stay outside, so I left her with her monkeys and I went in. This cave was much bigger than Virupaksha, and even though there may have been ten or twelve people in it, I had no problem finding a spot to meditate. I didn't want to leave Maddie for too long, so after a fifteen or twenty-minute meditation I came out and we started to make our way back down the mountain. We came down on a different path from the one we had walked up, and when we got to the bottom, we seemed to be a mile or so from the ashram. It was starting to get dark, so we hopped into a tuk-tuk, one of those three-wheel auto rickshaws that are all over India, for a ride back to the ashram so we could grab our shoes, get some dinner, and head back to our hotel for the night.

The next day we went back to the ashram, as I wanted to spend some more time walking the grounds and checking the place out. I went into the Old Hall, the building where Sri Bhagavan spent most of his later years, and sat for a few minutes of meditation. Most of Sri Bhagavan's talks, talks that I had read so many times over the years, took place here, and it just felt good to be in the same room where so many people from all over the world and from all walks of life had come to be in the presence of this enlightened being, and to receive the blessings of the silence of the Absolute that emanated from him. Before leaving, we went into the ashram bookstore and I picked up a few books on Sri Ramana Maharshi that I hadn't seen before. Our driver then took Maddie and me to a beach resort on the Bay of Bengal, where we spent a few days before heading to Chennai (Madras) and our flight home to the States.

CHAPTER 22

Egypt

While Niki has learned and practiced Transcendental Meditation, the TM-Sidhi Program, Sudarshan Kriya, T'ai Chi, and qigong, she's not into it like I am. She prefers her yoga, tennis, and BodyPump. I've asked her to go with me to Bhutan, Nepal, and India, but she didn't have any interest. There was one place she was interested in going, and in November of 2010, thirty days before the start of the Arab Spring, we took a trip to Egypt, the land of the pharaohs. Wanting to see everything, we booked a two-week guided tour.

We spent our first night in Cairo. It was late in the afternoon when we arrived at our hotel, and we were told it would probably be best to have dinner in the hotel and rest up, as we would be leaving first thing in the morning to start our tour of Egypt. Niki and I went straight to our room, dropped off our bags, then went back downstairs, out the front door, and jumped in a taxi. We told the driver to take us to the Khan el-Khalili, the famous bazaar located in the Islamic district of Cairo. When we got there the place was hopping. This huge, chaotic, open-air market was built in the fourteenth century and had everything from hookahs to belly dancing outfits, from gold and silver jewelry to antiques and leather goods. We found a little restaurant that didn't seem too touristy, grabbed some dinner, then walked around. The market was jammed with people, shops, coffeehouses, and restaurants, and it had a great vibe. We picked up a few trinkets for friends back home, then hopped in a cab for the ride back to our hotel.

The next morning we headed to Hurghada, a tourist resort on the Red Sea. Our tour group was maybe sixty people and when we traveled by road, as we did to Hurghada, it was in two large tour buses. I'm a real water person, and our hotel was right on the Red Sea. I went down to the boat docks to see if I could rent a boat but was told they don't rent boats; we would have to hire a boat with a captain, who would then take us out. I told the guy that would be fine and asked which ones were available. He pointed to one boat and said we could hire that one; a boat that was about 100 feet long and looked like it could hold over 150 people.

I said, "I don't think so, there's just the two of us; what's the smallest boat available?" He then pointed to a dive boat that was a little over thirty feet long and could hold maybe twenty-five people. I said fine, and the next day we went out. We sailed up and down the coast, seeing the waterfront as it's meant to be seen: From the water. We passed dozens of gorgeous yachts, both anchored out in the Red Sea and tied up in marinas. We stopped at a reef and did some snorkeling, and after a few hours of sightseeing, our captain drove us back to the docks.

The next day we rented a dune buggy to go out with a group into the Eastern Desert, that part of the Sahara Desert that lies between the Nile River to the west and the Red Sea to the east. Our destination was a small Bedouin village that was established miles out in the desert. We had dinner out there and got to ride some camels, and then headed back to town. The next morning we left Hurghada, heading out to see the great sights of Egypt.

Several years prior to our trip, I had read a very interesting book, *A Search in Secret Egypt*, by Paul Brunton. I first came across Paul Brunton while reading about Sri Ramana Maharshi. Brunton was born in London in 1898. At an early age he developed an interest in occultism and started on a lifelong quest for truth, a quest that first took him to India where he interviewed hundreds of mystics, gurus, spiritualists, and magicians. Paul Brunton's search eventually led him to Sri Ramana Maharshi, who later became his guru. Brunton was a writer and journalist by trade and in 1934 published his first book, *A Search in Secret India*. This widely read book was referred to many times in the books that I was reading on the life and teaching of Sri Ramana Maharshi, and I picked up a copy.

Paul Brunton was an eloquent writer whose poetic, descriptive style drew me in and gave me the sense that I was there along with him on his many spiritual journeys; journeys which, though some seventy years earlier, I found very similar to mine. Over the years Brunton wrote eleven books on his search for truth, and I have read them all. I enjoy reading from an actual physical copy of a book, and I found myself so attracted to Brunton's writings, and the sense that I was back in time with him, that whenever

141

possible I purchased first editions of his books. My copy of his third book, *A Search in Secret Egypt*, is a first edition that was published in 1936.

Paul Brunton's search for truth took him from India to Egypt, where his research led him to believe that the Egyptian ancient temples, in addition to having public areas used for worship by the masses, had special, isolated buildings wherein high priests performed secret mystical rituals for a select few; rituals which gave these select few an experience of the afterlife and thus a true knowledge of the Self. These were rituals wherein a person was put into a death-like trance, causing their soul to leave the body. These initiates were then brought back to life, giving the "Born Again" the true knowledge that there is no death. The Egyptians called these rites the "Mysteries" and those who went through these initiations, who were very few, were sworn to absolute secrecy to never reveal what passed within those secret chambers. Paul Brunton believed that Moses himself was one of the select few who received this death-trance initiation, thus conferring on him this sacred knowledge.

Reading Paul Brunton's *A Search in Secret Egypt* gave me some insights as to what might have actually been going on in ancient Egypt. We were about to visit what may be considered the world's most magnificent structures; structures that were built many thousands of years ago by a civilization which I believe we still know very little about. Not that there isn't a lot known about ancient Egypt; there is. But my interests have always been in knowing the underlying truth, the Ultimate Truth, and not the apparent truth that first meets the eye. It appeared to me that these monumental structures may not have been constructed by powerful, egotistical rulers interested only in their own self-gratification and final resting places, but rather, they may have been built to help transport the awareness, in some unknown way, of a select few initiates into the Absolute and then back again, thus giving them a knowledge of the Ultimate Truth, the truth that we are not these mortal bodies born only to die and then, hopefully, to somehow be resurrected in an eternal paradise, but rather, we are a timeless consciousness that never came into existence and will never cease to be. Whatever the truth may be regarding this ancient Egyptian society and their fantastic structures, it does not change the Ultimate Truth, which is ever-existent and never-changing.

Niki and I traveled all through Egypt. We visited the Valley of the Kings, took a four-day boat trip down the Nile (stopping to see all the historical sites along the way), and flew to Abu Simbel, the site of the Great Temple of Ramses II. This temple was carved out of a mountainside in the thirteenth century BC. Over the passage of time, this temple fell into disuse and eventually became covered by sand, only to be rediscovered in 1813. It has been said that if those compiling the list of the Seven Wonders of the Ancient World had been aware of this sand-hidden temple, they would have included it on their list.

Our final stop on our tour of Egypt was once again Cairo, where we spent several days. We traveled all over the city, taking in as many sights as we could. In addition to seeing the museums, bazaars, and all the touristy stuff, Niki and I took taxis or public transportation to some of the neighborhoods and got out and just walked around, thus gaining a real feel for the city and its people. When we walked around Cairo at night, which we did a lot, Niki would wear a scarf on her head to show respect for the culture and to not draw any unwanted attention our way.

One place I particularly wanted to see was Coptic Cairo, the center of Egypt's Coptic Christian community. The Christian Coptic church, most likely the oldest Christian church in the world, was based on the teaching of Saint Mark, one of the original twelve apostles of Jesus who brought Christianity to Egypt in 42 AD. The Coptic beliefs and understandings of the teachings of Jesus differed somewhat from those of the Catholic church, and during the fifth century, in an attempt to consolidate authority, the Coptic church was exiled. The Catholic church not only exiled those who disagreed with any of their doctrines; they also banned and wanted destroyed any writing that may have gone against any of their teachings, or contradicted in any way the four Gospels that the church chose for inclusion in the Bible. Egypt was a great seat of learning, and their Christian libraries contained volumes of early writing on Christianity. The Coptics, in an attempt to protect their Christian texts, placed a collection of these writings in an earthen jar that was then sealed and buried. In 1945, this jar was discovered near the upper Egyptian town of Nag Hammadi. In it were thirteen leather-bound ancient papyrus codices that contained third- and fourth-century translations of early Christian writing from Greek to Coptic. This collection of Gnostic Scriptures, which includes the Gospel of Thomas, the Gospel of Mary, and the Gospel of Judas, is known as the Nag Hammadi Library.

We took the Cairo Metro to Coptic Cairo, as it was well outside of the downtown area where we were staying. We visited several of the old Coptic churches, including the Church of the Virgin Mary, also known as the Hanging Church, as it was built on top of, and hangs over, some ancient Roman towers. This church, believed to have been built in the seventh century, was the most famous Coptic Christian church in Cairo, and we found it to also be the most beautiful. Like the Buddhist monasteries I had visited in Bhutan, this ancient church had a wonderful spiritual feeling, a feeling of silence and stillness.

Included in our guided tour of the Cairo area was, of course, a trip to the Great Pyramid of Giza, the oldest and only remaining of the Seven Wonders of the Ancient World. The Great Pyramid is the oldest and largest of the three pyramids in the Giza pyramid complex. It was constructed using 2.3 million blocks of limestone, each weighing approximately 2.5 tons. It was early afternoon when our bus pulled up to the complex, and our tour guide told us that we could walk all around the area, but we could not go into any of the pyramids, as they only allow 300 visitors a day and tickets were not available. I walked over to one of the guards standing outside of the Great Pyramid and asked him where the ticket office was, and he pointed to a building several hundred yards away. I told Niki to stay put and that I would go see if I could get us some tickets, and then I took off, sprinting to the ticket building. As I approached the building, I saw that there was a fence around it. Not wanting to waste any time running around to the opening, I hopped the fence. Once inside, I walked up to the ticket window and asked for two tickets to enter the Great Pyramid, and yes, I got two tickets. I hopped the fence again and sprinted back to Niki.

The entrance to the Great Pyramid was nothing more than a small opening fifty-six feet up from the ground. We went in and immediately had to navigate our way through a passage that was only about three feet high and three feet wide and descended for about sixty feet at a twenty-six–degree angle. This passage was so low that to get through it we had to put our hands on our knees and crouch down. After traversing this passageway, we came to another one that was the same height and width and that ascended at a twenty-six–degree angle for 129 feet. This ascending passageway brought us to the Grand Gallery, another ascending passage that was 153 feet long. But instead of crouching over, we could walk upright, as this seven-foot-wide passage was twenty-eight feet high. It was truly amazing to come into this giant opening in the middle of this mammoth pyramid.

As we ascended to the top of the Grand Gallery, we came to an antechamber that led to a room known as the King's Chamber, a thirty-four–foot by seventeen-foot room with a nineteen-foot high flat ceiling located in the heart of the pyramid. And while the rest of the pyramid was constructed of 2.5-ton limestone blocks, this room was constructed of massive solid red granite blocks, with the blocks used for the ceiling of this chamber weighing between 50 to 80 tons each. The entire inside of the pyramid had a silent feel to it, but this room had a strange feeling of dead silence; a silence and stillness that gave the sense that we were totally cut off from the rest of the world. Niki and I were all alone in this room, which was empty except for a sarcophagus that was carved from a single block of red granite. Or rather, Niki and I *thought* we were all alone in this room. As we walked across the room toward the sarcophagus, a guy started to climb out of it. This guy was from Australia and was excited—really excited. He could hardly contain himself. He told us that he had been lying in the sarcophagus with his eyes closed and had just had some kind of fantastic experience. He couldn't describe it to us; he just said that we had to get in and see for ourselves.

This guy left the room, and Niki climbed into the sarcophagus. She lay down for a couple of minutes and then got out. She said it was very peaceful and relaxing, but nothing earth-shattering. I then climbed in. The sarcophagus was cut from a single block of red granite and weighed an estimated 3.75 tons. Its interior dimensions were about seventy-seven inches in length, twenty-six inches in width, and thirty-four inches in depth. It appeared that it once had had a lid. The reason that the sarcophagus was still in the King's Chamber was that it was too big to be removed, as it couldn't fit through the doorway or passages, meaning that it had to have been placed in this chamber before the ceiling was put in place. Although this room is known as the King's Chamber, no mummy was ever found there or anywhere else in the Great Pyramid, and it is unknown if this pyramid was even intended as a burial place. Additionally, the King's Chamber was built with two airshafts, something no mummy would ever have needed. These shafts point to certain stars at various times of the year, and some believe that they may have been constructed for astrological purposes.

Paul Brunton believed that the Great Pyramid was constructed not as a tomb, but as a temple to be used by the high priests in their performance of the "mysteries." In *A Search in Secret Egypt*, he writes about the time he was given permission to spend the night alone in the King's Chamber. Upon arriving, the guards opened the gates to the entrance of the pyramid, then locked them behind him as he entered for his twelve-hour overnight stay. Brunton used a torch to make his way through the pyramid to the King's Chamber. Upon reaching the room, he extinguished his torch and sat in total darkness, describing the atmosphere as "psychic." As he sat in the room with eyes closed, he felt some type of evil force with phantom forms moving across the room. This quite unnerving experience was later followed by visions of benevolent high priests in white robes who approached him. An older priest told him to get into the sarcophagus and lie down, which he did. He was then passed through sensations of dying and leaving his body, only to be later brought back into his body with the priest telling him, "Thou hast now learned the great lesson. Man, whose soul was born out of the Undying, can never really die."

In 1799, Napoleon spent the night alone in the King's Chamber of the Great Pyramid. When he emerged the next morning, it was reported that he was visibly shaken. When asked by an aide if he had witnessed anything mysterious, he replied that he had no comment and that he never wanted the incident mentioned again. Years later, while on his deathbed, Napoleon was asked again by a friend what really happened that night in the pyramid. He was about to tell him and stopped. Then he shook his head and said, "No, what's the use? You would never believe me." Napoleon never told anyone what happened that night in the pyramid.

As I lay down in the sarcophagus, I didn't know what to expect, but one thing was for certain: I wasn't at all concerned with evil forces or visions of phantoms. This may sound strange, but when I sit down to meditate, I always feel totally protected with a sense that nothing bad could ever happen to me. Occasionally when I meditate, I will have some vision (usually some unknown person or face that I see), but really, this almost never happens. If it does, I treat the vision with total dispassion. Not textbook dispassion, but meditation dispassion; I don't care if it's happening and I don't care if it's not happening: I just pay no attention to it. As I lay there on my back with my arms to my sides, I just closed my eyes and let go. The pyramid, the King's Chamber, and the sarcophagus all came together to create an overwhelming atmosphere of silence and stillness, and I immediately felt the boundaries of my body dissolve as I expanded infinitely out into space. I've had this experience many, many times before during meditation, and also during my qigong practice, but this was different. Usually there is some sense that I am where I am and from that location I just dissolve and spread out in every direction. Here, however, I did not have the sense that I was lying in the sarcophagus in the King's Chamber in the Great Pyramid and expanding out in every direction. Here, I had the sense that I was in outer space, nowhere near where I was, nowhere near Earth, nowhere near anything. I was just out there somewhere in empty space, expanding in all directions into that empty space;

an empty space that was me. And unlike meditation where I am meditating, or qigong where I am doing qigong, here I was doing nothing. Nothing except lying still with my eyes closed and letting go. Everything that I was experiencing, everything that was happening, was being caused just by me being in the sarcophagus. The pyramid, with its construction, location, and orientation, along with the construction, location, and orientation of the King's Chamber with the sarcophagus in it, caused these sensations. I could see how someone, no matter what their level of experience or lack thereof, could have some pretty amazing experiences by doing the same, just lying in the sarcophagus, and for the uninitiated, I could see how those experiences could possibly be frightening.

I'm not sure how long I stayed there—not long; maybe five minutes. For some reason, maybe because I was in the Great Pyramid, as I was getting up, I kept my eyes closed and lifted my arms up straight and sat up as stiff as a board, just like the mummies do in the movies. Immediately I heard a bloodcurdling scream. I opened my eyes to an Asian man who was peering down at me from over the side of the sarcophagus. I had thought that I was still alone in the room with Niki, but I was wrong. Unbeknownst to me, a group of Asian tourists had entered the King's Chamber, and just as I was sitting up (in my best mummy impersonation), one fellow came over to look in. He quickly realized that I wasn't a mummy returning from the dead, as he grabbed his chest and started laughing.

Niki and I made our way out of the pyramid and walked around a bit to observe it from the outside. It was massive, and to think that it had been built 4,500 years ago by some ancient civilization was just mind-boggling. We met up with our group at the bus and told everyone that we got to go inside the pyramid, and it seemed that we were the only ones who did. We then drove over to see the Great Sphinx of Giza, which was only a mile away.

A sphinx is a mythical creature with the head of a human and the body of a lion. We have all seen pictures of the Great Sphinx of Giza, but I was unprepared for how massive it is: 241 feet long and taller than a six-story building. The Sphinx is a statue that was carved over 4,500 years ago from a single mass of bedrock limestone. We weren't able to get right up to the Sphinx, as they were doing restoration work and it was fenced off, but as with the Great Pyramid, seeing this in person was breathtaking. The origins of the Sphinx are still very much a mystery. Why was it made, and when was it made? As with the pyramids, no one knows.

The next day we had our last tour, a trip to the Pyramid of Djoser, the oldest pyramid in Egypt, built during the twenty-seventh century BC in Saqqara, an ancient burial ground located about nineteen miles south of Cairo. The Pyramid of Djoser is a step pyramid, a structure that uses flat platforms, or steps, that recede from the ground up. While this seven-step pyramid was nowhere near as large as the Great Pyramid of Giza, it was still a very large structure (203 feet tall verses 455 feet for the Great Pyramid). At the time of our visit, Cairo was experiencing one of their worst sandstorms in years (bad enough that they had to close the airport), and not a lot of people wanted to go on this tour to Saqqara. When we got there, Niki and I were the only ones who really wanted to walk around and see the place, and our guard said that he would walk around with us.

On our tour bus, and on every tour bus that we saw, there were three people who were not tourists: The driver, the tour guide, and the guard. Our tour guide was a university-trained Egyptologist who really knew his stuff. Our guard was a man in a suit who carried a sidearm and a submachine gun. Tourism is one of Egypt's main sources of income, and the government wants to ensure that tourists are kept safe. We never felt unsafe anywhere in Egypt, but we were happy to have our guard with us as we walked around Saqqara. The next day, Niki and I flew back home.

PART TWO

THE DISCOVERY

Discovery: Something found that
had not been known before.

CHAPTER 23

Buried Treasure

Let me ask you a question: Do you have a back-yard where you live? If not, assume that you do. My question is: Why aren't you out in your backyard, digging for buried treasure? Really, this is not a trick question; why aren't you digging for buried treasure in your backyard? The reason you aren't digging for buried treasure in your backyard is because there isn't any treasure buried in your backyard or, more correctly, you don't *believe* that there is any treasure buried in your backyard. Now let's just say that you buy a house on ten acres in the Bahamas. This house is really old, over 300 years old, and like most really old houses, your house has no closets. You decide to tear down part of a wall to build a closet and when you do, you find a very old leather pouch that was hidden in the wall. Inside this pouch is a 300-year-old treasure map that says that there is a treasure box with 2,000 gold doubloons in it buried in the backyard of your house, next to a stream and by a big rock. You look out into the backyard and you see a stream and a big rock, and you are 100 percent sure that the treasure map you just found is real, and you are absolutely positive that there is a treasure box buried in your backyard. What are you going to do? I'll tell you what you're going to do: You're going to grab a shovel and you're going to start digging, and you're not going to stop digging until you find that buried treasure.

Why don't people sit quietly every day and meditate? Why don't people go inside to look for that buried treasure that is hidden inside of them? It's because they don't believe that there is anything inside. Or maybe they believe that there might be something inside, but how could it be as great, as attractive, as all the wonderful things on the outside that their senses are experiencing every day? One very famous person knew that there was a treasure buried deep inside of everyone, a treasure greater than all the treasures in the world, and he clearly stated so 2,000 years ago saying, "For, behold, the kingdom of God is within you."

So what have I discovered from my lifelong search for truth? Well I really haven't discovered anything, which is actually quite a find! For while I have uncovered that secret buried treasure chest and opened it up and looked inside, I found that it was empty. But, and there are no words to accurately convey this, I found the wonderment of everything in that emptiness. And yes, this has been quite an important discovery in my quest for truth, for you see, when I first started on my search to find out what it's all about, I thought that I was looking for "something," something that could be found and then added to my collection of things that I had learned, or obtained, as I passed through this life; another feather for my cap, if you will. But what I discovered was that there is nothing to find and no one to find it. There just "is," and this finding is the mother lode.

What I came to understand during my search for truth was that what I was looking for was self-realization, the answer to the question: "Who am I?" To move toward my goal I would need a means, a path. I chose my own path, which is not to say that I created a new path. On the contrary—I chose and followed ancient teachings and methods; teachings and methods that I believed would fit my personality. And while my inward enthusiasm has never waned, my outward actions may appear changed, as I now move forward with more of a sense of ease. I did not leave my mind at the door as I moved along on my journey, as you need your mind to go beyond the mind. The mind comes along 100 percent; you just need to be open and prepared to drop all preconceived ideas, and know that at some point you must abandon your mind, as there can be no expectation of comprehending the incomprehensible. Removal of ignorance is the aim of our practice, not the acquisition of realization, as realization is ever-present. If realization is something to be acquired, then it must be understood to have been absent at one time and present at another, and this is just not the case. As I stated in my introduction, the Ultimate Truth is changeless. It is always true and not bound by limitations of time and space. There is no reality or unreality to be discovered. There is just understanding—understanding according to your own level of wisdom.

The Ultimate Truth must encompass everything, including contradictions. If you only have one point of view, and not its polar opposite, then you are putting boundaries on the truth, a truth that has no boundaries. But this is only for relative discussions; in the Absolute, boundaries or no boundaries has no meaning. The truth and wisdom that you seek is not found in scriptures or in the words of holy men, as these contain only descriptions of the Absolute, along with directions as to where this great treasure is to be found: Inside, where it has always been. Don't get hung up on the descriptions of the Self; the value lies in the road map, the directions as to how to realize the Truth. Find it (or, more correctly, remember it, as it is never lost) on the inside, and you will see that it is your own true being, and that it is not just inside, but it is, and always has been, everywhere and nowhere.

If you prefer to use the word "God" over the word "Truth" as you contemplate the Absolute, fine: There isn't only one God or many Gods—there is only God; God did not *create* the universe, God *became* the universe, and, as such, this world which is born of God, is not different from God; God doesn't come into our life—God is life.

CHAPTER 24

Moving Forward

What is it that everyone is looking for? It's happiness. Everyone wants to be happy, and people spend their lives looking for it. They look for it in everything around them: Their family and friends, their jobs, sports, hobbies, travel, gaining fame and fortune—everything. We find happiness in so many things, but the happiness we find always seems to be fleeting. No matter how great something is, no matter how happy it makes us feel, that feeling of happiness is never constant; it has its ups and downs. Take your favorite food for example. Let's say that your favorite food is chocolate. You love chocolate, but what would happen if the only food you could eat for the next week was chocolate? You had to eat it for breakfast, lunch, and dinner, and not just a little; you had to eat a lot of it. You'd be lucky if you could get through one day before you got sick of chocolate and never wanted to see it again. And what if your life was seemingly perfect? How many people do we hear about who appear to have it all: Money, family, friends, good health—everything, and yet they are unhappy? Why? Because they still have the feeling that there is something missing in their lives. They are not sure what it is; just that there is the sense that something is missing. What is it? It's inner peace. A peace that comes not from external sources, but rather one that just naturally springs up from within.

We think that everything is happening on the outside. We believe that the people and things around us are what are making us happy or sad, filling us with joy, or stirring up anger, when in truth everything is happening on the inside. Let me give you an example. Imagine that, God forbid, you get a phone call and it's the police and they inform you that your best friend has just died in a car accident. You hang up the phone. How do you feel? You are distraught, beside yourself with grief. A few minutes go by and your phone rings again. You pick it up, and on the other end of the line is your supposedly dead friend. Your friend tells you that they are fine. They were just making a video for YouTube, and they took their old car and pushed it up against a tree and put a dummy in the driver's seat and set the car on fire for the YouTube video, but no one was hurt and they are perfectly okay. You hang up the phone. How do you feel? You feel fantastic. What just actually happened? Your sadness and subsequent happiness came about solely because of your thoughts, your state of mind. Your first thoughts were that your friend was dead; then your thoughts changed to your friend is okay. Nothing changed on the outside; everything happened on the inside. Only your thoughts changed.

What makes us angry or upset? It's always the same thing: We want people to act in a certain way and when they don't, we get upset. We want the cashier at the food store to say thank you when we give them our money. They don't, and we get upset. We want the driver who just cut us off in traffic to be a courteous, safe driver. They aren't, and we are upset. We want our kids to study hard in school and to do well. They don't, and we are upset. Or we want a situation to be a certain way, and it's not. We want the weather to be nice for a big family picnic. It ends up pouring rain, and we are bummed out. We want our favorite politician to get elected. They don't, and we are upset. If we would accept people and situations as they are, we could save ourselves a lot of mental anguish. It's not that we just sit back idly and never take action. We don't. We take appropriate action when necessary, but we accept the situation as it is. If I see someone robbing my neighbor's house, I don't get mad at the person because they are a robber. No, I accept that the person is a robber, but I do call the police so they can come and arrest them.

You walk down the sidewalk and someone bumps into you. They then push you out of the way and yell at you to watch where you're going. What's going on with this person? For whatever reason, this person is uptight and totally stressed-out. Or you bump into someone else and they say, "Oh, I'm sorry. Are you okay?" What's going on with this person? They are relaxed with a low level of stress.

We think that everything is happening on the outside, but really it's all happening on the inside. How we are on the inside, our level of centeredness, our level of stress, our level of consciousness, affects how we act in the world, and how the world affects us. The world is our teacher and it is there to help us reach higher states of consciousness, if we only have the awareness of what is actually going on. We think that some mean and nasty person is causing us to be upset when, in reality, it is we who is letting this person upset us. If the world seems hard and is always pushing on you, this is your tension and stiffness giving it something to push on. It's not that we are never going to get upset; we are. But we take note of what is happening, and we have the awareness of what is going on and why. We don't try not to be upset. We don't pretend we're not upset; that's just mood-making. Our goal is to actually not get upset, and this happens as our level of consciousness rises as we move forward on our journey to find the Ultimate Truth, enlightenment, or whatever label we choose to put on it. It's not that things will never have an effect on us; they will, but it will be more like a line on water. At a lower-level, stressed-out state of consciousness, everything is a big deal. Something upsetting happens to us, and it is like taking a chisel to a piece of granite. It makes a line, a permanent mark, and it stays with us for a long time. Whereas with a higher level, stress-free state of consciousness, when something upsetting happens to us, it is more like a line on water that we make with our finger. The line is there, and then it quickly vanishes. It's had its effect, but only at a very superficial level. It's there; then it's gone. One thing I like to say to people who seem to be upset by what I see as something very minor is to apply the five-year rule: How will this affect you in five years? Not only will most of these "terribly" upsetting things not bother us in five years; in five years we won't even remember them.

This reminds me of the story of two monks in ancient Japan. The monks are celibate and have nothing to do with women. In fact, in their order, they never even touch women. One day they are riding their horses in the countryside when they come to a river. At the river is a young woman who is standing on the bank trying to cross, but the current is too strong. As the monks go to cross the river, one of them leans over and grabs the woman and picks her up and carries her across on his horse. When he reaches the other side, he sets her down and continues riding. The other monk sees this and is very upset. He tries to contain himself, but he can't. After several miles he finally says to his friend, "I can't believe it."

His friend says, "What?"

He says, "Not only did you touch that woman; you picked her up and held her tight to you as you carried her across that river. I just can't believe it."

His friend replies, "Oh, that woman. Are you still carrying her? I left her back at the river."

CHAPTER 25

Choosing a Path

If you think there may be something worth check-ing out, something on the "inside" to go along with all the stuff on the "outside," the stuff that you perceive through your senses, where do you begin? Let's say that you decide that you want to become a world-class runner. You sit on the couch all day long, watching TV, drinking beer, and eating bon bons, all the while saying to yourself that you want to be a world-class runner. I have a strong suspicion that this is not going to work, not going to get you to your goal. If you really want to become a world-class runner, you're going to need to go out and buy some sneakers, put them on, hit the streets, and start running. Same thing with spiritual pursuits: If you really want to find out what's it all about, if you think there may be this thing called en-lightenment, self-realization, or whatever, and you would like to "attain" it, or at least explore it, you will need to do something. You need to take action: Put on your sneakers, choose a "path," and get on it.

What path should you choose and how much time should you put into this endeavor? Let's regroup for a moment: You need to choose a path to lead you to the Ultimate Truth, self-realization—this thing called "enlightenment." While all paths are in the domain of the relative and not difficult to understand, enlightenment is in the domain of the Absolute, and not only is it difficult to understand, it is impossible to understand, as all understanding takes place in the mind, and the Absolute is beyond mind, beyond intellect. To make things even more challenging, the Absolute is not a "thing" to be found or acquired, and although all things are included in it, and there is no place where it does not exist; there is no "place" where it will be found. Yes, the path to enlightenment is arduous and has been analogized to "walking the razor's edge," but it can also be looked at like this: The Ultimate Truth exists everywhere, and although it can never be found (as it is never lost), all paths lead to it.

First a caveat: I am not an enlightened master by any stretch of the imagination. There are many paths to choose from, and I can only speak from my own experiences. That being said, there are two things that lead you toward enlightenment: Knowledge and experience. It is like two sides of the same coin; one hand washes the other, if you will. Knowledge brings experience, and experience brings knowledge. For me, the most important thing for gaining experience is to have a daily meditation practice. You need to learn to meditate. When I say this to some people, they will say, "Oh, gardening is my meditation," or, "Running is my meditation." While gardening or running may have a calming effect, they are not the same as meditating. Meditation not only calms the mind; it leads you to beyond the mind and into the silent depths of the transcendence. So what meditation technique should you choose? This is a very personal decision. I prefer ancient meditation practices, things that have been around for a long time. I'm not that into the New Age stuff. There are lots of practices to choose from. I am familiar with both Transcendental Mediation and the Art of Living's Sahaj Samadhi Meditation, and highly recommend both. These are mantra-based meditations that are taught by certified teachers from the respective organizations.

There are also many other meditation techniques out there for you to choose from. The Self-Realization Fellowship, founded by Paramahansa Yogananda, teaches meditation, as does the Society in the Abidance of Truth, a group that follows the teachings of Sri Ramana Maharshi. There are also many Buddhist and Zen Buddhist organizations teaching meditation. You can also learn a Mindfulness Meditation from a variety of sources. The prophet Muhammad meditated consistently, and for those of the Islamic faith, the Sufi order might be a good place to look for guidance on meditation.

Meditation is not religion. It is just a technique to settle the mind, causing thoughts to drop away, thus leaving one with a transcendental experience. Transcendental Meditation and the Art of Living's Sahaj Samadhi Meditation have both been passed down through a long lineage of masters, and both are taught only by highly trained, certified teachers. It is said that meditation techniques learned this way, through qualified teachers, carry with them the grace of the entire line of masters. Is this true? That's not for me to say. The grace of the Absolute is there for the benefit of all, and it is not directed to any particular person or group. Whether one is open to receiving this grace is another matter.

There is a story from ancient Hinduism about a king who wanted to learn to meditate. Knowing that one of his ministers meditated, the king summoned him into his chambers so that the minister could teach him. When the king asked the minister to teach him to meditate, the minister told him he could not do so, as he was not a qualified teacher. The king said he did not care; he just wanted to learn to meditate, and he wanted the minister to instruct him. The minister explained to the king that meditation is passed down through a long line of masters, and through this lineage a grace is passed, thus giving the mantra its power. But this grace is only passed if the teacher is qualified. If not, the mantra will not be effective. The king did not want to hear any of this, and he demanded that the minister teach him immediately. With this, the minister looked across the room to the king's guards and yelled, "Guards! Arrest the king and throw him in the dungeon!"

The bewildered king looked at the minister and said, "What are you doing?" He then turned to his guards and said, "Guards! Arrest the minister!" The guards immediately sprang to action and grabbed the minister. With this, the minister started to laugh. The king gave him an odd look and demanded to know why he was laughing.

The minister said, "Don't you see? We both just said the exact same thing to the guards. I told them to arrest you, and you told them to arrest me. However, when I spoke, my words had no authority behind them and therefore had no effect on the guards. When you spoke, the guards reacted immediately, as your words had the authority of the king." Smiling, the king nodded. He understood.

So you learn to meditate, and you start meditating according to the instructions you have been given. I would say at the minimum, you want to meditate for twenty minutes, twice a day, seven days a week. If something comes up and you need to miss a meditation, so be it. But if you are determined, that should only happen sometime between very seldom and never.

The other side of the coin in your search for self-realization is knowledge. Where do you find knowledge? That's easy: It's everywhere. But again, I like reading the old stuff. But this is just my personality, my preference. I'm not suggesting that New Age stuff is not beneficial. If I'm not reading ancient scripture, I'm reading writings by or about people who I believe are enlightened, both past and present. I'll read anything that I believe will give me a little more insight, and include works from every religious tradition. I believe in casting a wide net. But truth be told, knowledge comes to us in many forms. Never assume that the spiritual master giving a lecture at the front of the auditorium will impart more knowledge to you than the janitor who is cleaning the bathrooms in the basement. And it might just be that, with a little reflection, that person who is driving you crazy and really upsetting you is your greatest teacher.

There is a story about a man who went up to the Buddha and told him that he wanted to get on the path to self-realization and asked what he should do. The Buddha told him to go back to his village and meet with each and every person, and embrace and accept each one just as they are, and then come back in one month and report to the Buddha. One month later he returned, telling the Buddha that he did as instructed and met with each member of his village, over 200 people, and he was able to accept each and every person just as they were, with only one exception. He explained to the Buddha that there was one person who was just an awful human being, someone who drove him crazy and whom he could not accept. He asked the Buddha to please make an exception in his case, as he had accepted over 200 people and there was only one whom he could not accept. The Buddha said yes, he would make an exception. He told the man he could go back to his village and that he did not have to accept every person—he only had to accept one—the person who was driving him crazy!

I now spend approximately three hours a day meditating. I spend another forty-five minutes or so a day doing yoga, T'ai Chi, and qigong, and I usually read for at least thirty minutes to an hour every night. I don't read so much anymore for gaining knowledge, as I have read so much for so many years; I mostly just read because I really enjoy reading scriptural and spiritual stuff. (I have compiled a reading list at the end of this book, with a few suggestions to get you started.) Added to my sadhana (spiritual practice) is my ongoing self-reflection.

So how much time should you spend on your endeavor? That's up to you. For me, I have the balance that I like and my lifestyle affords me.

There is a story about Cheng Man-ch'ing, the Chinese master who brought the Yang Short Style of T'ai Chi Ch'uan (the style that I practice) to the United States from

China in 1964. Cheng opened a school for T'ai Chi in New York City, and some of his more dedicated students were really practicing a lot. After several years, a few of these more dedicated students approached Cheng and told him that although they were practicing T'ai Chi for seven or eight hours a day, they were still not getting any closer to his level of skill. His reply was that that was because they were only practicing seven or eight hours per day, while he was practicing twenty-four hours a day.

The path you choose must fit your personality and your lifestyle; it should feel right for you. As you move along on your quest, don't get stuck by your beliefs, concepts, or revelations, for while the path is continuous, it is by no means straight. You must be easy with everything, for all knowledge, experience, and wisdom gained as you journey forward will eventually need to be dropped, as you don't gain the truth; you just let go of the false. The truth is not obtained: It is what remains. And how do you know if you're making progress? There's one sure way: Even the bad days are good!

CHAPTER 26

How to Meditate

While I am not a teacher of meditation, I can give you some tips and tell you how to do a mindfulness meditation. I still believe that everyone should learn to meditate from a qualified teacher.

Three general points of meditation are:
- You are not trying to learn or know anything,
- You don't *do* anything, and
- There is no "you."

You merely sit and let meditation happen. If possible, you want to meditate in a place that is clean, quiet, and private. If this is not possible, you can meditate anywhere. (I have meditated on an airplane where the passengers on both sides of me were talking back and forth to each other for the entire flight.) When doing your daily meditation practice at home, I would try to do it in the same spot whenever possible. You want to have your door shut with no pets in the room, as pets seem to be attracted to people meditating, and you may find that they end up sitting on you.

For a mindfulness meditation, you want to sit up as straight as you can, while at the same time being as comfortable as possible. It is very important that you are in a comfortable position. You can sit on a chair, a couch, a bed, the floor—anywhere that you can get comfortable. If you can sit in a cross-legged position, that would be great. If not—no problem.

First I'll tell you what it is that you are going to be doing, and then I'll explain how to do it. Your attention will be on your breath and on the center of your chest. Sit comfortably and close your eyes. Totally relax every muscle in your body, including those in your face; just let everything go. This is not the time to solve any of your problems. This is your time to be alone with yourself. Become aware of your breath. Feel the air coming in through your nostrils, down your throat, and into the center of your chest. As effortlessly as possible, keep your attention on this passage of air for maybe thirty seconds to a minute: The air coming in your nostrils, down your throat, and into your chest; and the air leaving your chest, going up your throat, and out your nostrils. Now just let your attention go to the center of your chest and be aware of the air coming in and out of your chest as your chest rises and falls. This will be your meditation: Just gently and effortlessly resting your attention in the center of your chest with a slight awareness of the breath coming in and out. Do this meditation for twenty minutes. When you are done, stop meditating, and, with your eyes still closed, continue to sit or lie down for at least three or four minutes. After that, you're finished. That's it.

But there is so much more to this. As you are meditating, whatever you are doing is too much. Everything should be done as effortlessly and gently as possible, with just the slightest intention behind it. You are not trying to hold your attention on your chest or breath; you just gently and effortlessly bring it there and let go. There is no concentration. You just have a faint idea (and not necessarily a clear thought) of letting your attention rest quietly in the center of your chest. If you become aware (have thoughts) that your attention is not on the center of your chest, you just gently bring it back. You are not interested in keeping a conscious awareness of your chest. You just start your meditation by gently placing your attention on the center of the chest, being aware of the movement of the air coming in and out, and then let go, only to bring your attention back to the center of our chest if you become aware that it is not there. There is no effort.

Again, you are not trying to do anything or accomplish anything when you meditate. You are not attempting to feel something or learn anything. You are dispassionate about all that happens. This is meditation dispassion. You simply ignore anything and everything that may or may not be happening. You don't care if it is happening, and you don't care if it is not happening. Meditation releases stress, and as a byproduct of stress release thoughts can pop up. You are not trying to stop thoughts from arising. You are not trying to get rid of your thoughts or push them out of your mind. You simply cease being interested. You ignore them, pay no attention to them, and, as effortlessly as possible, let your attention gently rest at the center of your chest.

As you do this, two types of thoughts may come up: Disconnected thoughts and connected thoughts. Disconnected thoughts are just random, unrelated thoughts. Pay no mind to these. Do nothing, for just as these thoughts come on their own, they go on their own. Connected thoughts have a common theme; for example: *We are having friends over for dinner tomorrow; I think I'll bake a cake. Do I have flour? Yes, I think so. I know I'll need to buy some eggs. I know I need nuts. Where is the cake pan?*—and on and on and on. Just like disconnected thoughts, we do not care if we have connected thoughts, but as soon as we become aware of this rambling, we just let go and effortlessly bring our attention back to the center of our chest and our breath. Stay relaxed and let go. As thoughts settle during meditation, you may start to become aware of an all-pervading, ever-existing, pure awareness. When this happens, let your individual awareness rest in this pure awareness. With no effort at all on your part, these two awarenesses merge, leaving us with that which has always been.

You want the place where you meditate to be as quiet as you can make it, but as to any noises that are beyond your control, you just don't care. You accept all outside noises and let them pass right though you. Relax and let go, and let your body and mind just dissolve into space. As far as the time goes, have a clock across the room or a watch in front of you and try to place it in a spot where all you have to do to see it is open your eyes. You don't want to have to move around or even turn your head to check on the time. If you are going to meditate for twenty minutes, at some point in time a thought that the twenty minutes has passed will pop up. When it does, gently open your eyes, look at the clock, and then close your eyes. If twenty minutes or more have gone by, stop meditating and go into your rest period. If it's been less than twenty minutes, keep meditating. Always give yourself enough time to include a minimum of three or four minutes of rest after you have finished meditating. This is very important. If for some reason an emergency pops up and you need to stop meditating, when the emergency is over, go back and meditate for a few minutes and then do your rest.

When you meditate, your whole system slows down and you need to give your body time to stabilize before you go back to activity. Jumping up without stabilizing first can be a real shock to your system and may make you feel a little off. If possible, give yourself plenty of time for your meditation. If you are on a time schedule to do something or go somewhere, you may be worried that your meditation might go over the twenty minutes, and this could affect your ability to let go during your meditation.

It's best to meditate twice a day, morning and evening, and on an empty stomach. Before breakfast and before dinner is a good time, but if your schedule doesn't allow for this, just meditate at whatever time works best for you. You are not trying to stay awake when you meditate: If you fall asleep, you fall asleep. But meditation is not the time for sleep. If you find that you are falling asleep a lot when you meditate, then you are too tired and you need to be more rested before you meditate. Your morning meditation can be any time after 3:00 a.m., so if you wake up in the middle of night and you are having difficulty getting back to sleep, just wait until at least 3:00 a.m. and then meditate for twenty minutes and lie back down. You should easily fall asleep, going into a yogic sleep, which is a really nice deep sleep.

So what is a good meditation? Since we are not trying or wanting something to happen or not happen when we meditate, every meditation is good. Whatever is happening is what is supposed be happening. We are not trying to recreate some prior experience.

Imagine that you're a duck and you love all kinds of weather. You love sunny days and you love rainy days. You love it when the wind blows and you love it when it's still. You love hot days, warm days, and cold days. Now if you were a duck and I asked you, "How's the weather?" what are you going to say? You're going to say the weather is perfect, because you love it all. That's how you want to view your meditation: No matter what happens or doesn't happen, it's perfect. You are just being yourself; nothing else.

So what do you do when you're finished meditating? You don't do anything except live your life. Everything will happen from the inside out. You don't need to shave your head and wear sandals and an orange robe, but if that's what you want to do: Hey man, go for it. But really, meditation is like taking a shower. You take a shower in the morning, get dressed, and then go out and live your life. You don't go around all day saying, "I took a shower and I feel great."

Meditation is a tool to help give us an awareness of our true Self, to know our true nature. But we already are our true Self, our true nature; we are just forgetful. So the Self is not attained by doing anything other than remaining still and being as you are. By trying to move toward the Self, we are actually moving away. There is no "you" trying to obtain or experience something "else." There is no "other." There is no world outside of us; everything is happening within. This is the secret to meditation: You don't make progress through effort; you simply get still and sit there. The Self will show itself to you and bring you in. You don't do anything to get in. Just *"be still and know that I am God."*

Why is it said that by trying to move toward the Self, we are actually moving away? To answer this question, we need to look at how we perceive things. With external perception we need two conditions: We need the elimination of other perceptions (objects) and fixation on the one to be perceived. Of course we can perceive many things at the same time, and with multiple senses. For example, we can see, feel, and smell a campfire while at the same time talking to those sitting around it. But if our attention is truly focused on something, it is to the exclusion of other objects of perception.

With self-realization we only have one condition: The elimination of all perceptions. Since the pure consciousness that we seek is the Self, the "I," and not apart from the mind, concentration on it is not needed for its realization. We merely need thoughts to subside and then disappear, and the Self will be realized. Trying to get rid of thoughts does not work. We simply become uninterested, and the thoughts disappear on their own as a result of the meditation technique that we are using. Experience of the transcendence comes from mental purity, not concentration. As the only impurity of the mind is thought, ridding the mind of thought is to make it pure. So when we *try* to move toward the Self by concentration or intention, what we are actually doing is creating thoughts, which in turn moves us away from (obscures) the Self. There is no doing or trying. Just relax and let go. Surrender.

Meditation can promote creativity in us and sometimes this happens while we are meditating. What should we do if some earth-shattering thought comes up during our meditation, and we are afraid that we might forget it? Most of the songs on the Beatles' *White Album* were conceived during their course with Maharishi Mahesh Yogi in Rishikesh, India, in the spring of 1968. New songs kept popping up in John Lennon's head as he was meditating, and he didn't know what to do. Not wanting to forget the songs, he couldn't get the thoughts of them out of his head. He went to Maharishi and told him of his dilemma. Maharishi said it's very simple: Keep a pad and pen next to you when you meditate. When new songs come to you, just stop meditating and write the songs down. When done, just put the pad and pen back down and continue meditating.

CHAPTER 27

Benefits of Meditation

Not everyone is interested in self-realization, in discovering the Ultimate Truth, and that's fine, but does that mean that for those who aren't, meditation would not be useful? Not at all. Why do people brush their teeth? They do it to prevent cavities, whiten their teeth, have fresher breath, and to improve their overall health. But no matter the reason or reasons why one brushes their teeth, all the benefits are obtained. So if your only interest in brushing your teeth in the morning is to have fresh breath and prevent cavities, that's fine, but that brushing will still reduce your chances of having a heart attack or stroke. Meditation has many benefits, including stress release, better sleep, better heath, more focus, improved inter-personal relationships, and reaching higher states of consciousness. My sole purpose in learning to meditate was to obtain enlightenment. But what if one was to meditate for a lifetime, say sixty or seventy years, and not become enlightened. Does that mean that all that time meditating was spent in waste? Not at all. All of meditation's benefits are passed on to the meditator, no matter what the reason or reasons for taking it up. And as far as reaching higher states of consciousness goes, whether we are aware of it or not, progress is always made.

Normally the only way we really have to release stress is by sleeping. You're stressed out, you get a good night's sleep, and you wake up feeling better. The problem is, it's difficult to get a good night's sleep when you're totally stressed out. Meditation releases stress—big time. It releases more stress, and at much deeper levels, than sleep does. Removing stress from your nervous system strengthens it and helps it deal with future stresses. And again, what are some of the practical benefits of meditation besides releasing stress and sleeping better? How about preventing illnesses and improving all-around health, enhancing brain function, thus enabling us to better focus and solve problems, relieving anxiety, and enhancing emotional well-being.

The less stressed we are, the better we are able to handle every situation that comes our way. Imagine a husband comes home from work to his stay-at-home wife, who has been with their two young children all day. The husband walks in, and one of the kids acts up a little and the mom goes off the deep end. The kid's actions have no effect on the husband, and he asks his wife why she is so upset by what he sees as just normal kids' stuff. What's going on here? What's going on is that the mom has been with the kids all day and her stress level from dealing with them has reached its maximum capacity, and this last outburst is the proverbial straw that broke the camel's back. The dad, on the other hand, hasn't had to deal with the kids at all that day and his child-induced stress level is zero, so his kid's little outburst has no negative effect on him at all. So while the wife can just hang in there until the kids go to bed, her best bet would be for her husband to watch the kids while she goes off to the bedroom for a twenty-minute meditation. Not only will her remaining time with her husband and kids that evening be much more enjoyable, when she does go to bed for the night, she'll have a much-appreciated good night's sleep.

When are we short with our children (or parents)? When do we snap at our significant other or get into it with a friend or coworker? Is it when we are calm and relaxed? No, it's when we are stressed-out and uptight. The way we interact with others is directly related to our level of stress. High levels of stress bring about impatience, irritability, and rigidity. Low levels of stress promote a more easygoing, cheerful, flexible disposition.

Now you might be saying to yourself that you know that meditation would be good for you, and you would like to incorporate a daily meditation program into your life, but you just don't have the time. Well guess what? You don't have the time to *not* meditate! How's that? Meditation is beneficial to human physiology in so many ways, including brain function. The regular practice of meditation gives us a greater ability to focus and makes us more efficient in everything we do. So if you have concerns about lack of time, they are ill-founded, for you will find that the time spent in meditation is more than made up for by your increase in efficiency and productivity. And if better health, peace of mind, increased creativity, more focus, greater efficiency, and improved interpersonal relationships are not enough for you, let's add one more: Reversing the aging process.

Google that one and see what you find.

Meditating not only removes stress from your nervous system and raises your level of consciousness; it also has a very positive effect on those around you. Yes, your state of consciousness affects all who come into contact with you. Imagine you walk into a room. Sitting there are two men who, unbeknownst to you, are stressed-out bank robbers. You sit down next to them, and even though they do not say a word and they appear perfectly normal, you start to feel very uneasy. What's going on? What's going on is that their consciousness is having a negative effect on you. Now imagine you walk into another room with two men in it who are both dressed very normally and you sit down next to them. All of a sudden you start to experience an immense sense of well-being. Your mind settles and you feel a peace and expansion of consciousness like you have never felt before. You're overwhelmed almost to the point of tears, and you have no idea what's happening to you. The two men get up and leave the room, and someone else walks in and you inquire, "Who were those two men?"

The reply: "Those men? Oh, that was Jesus Christ and Siddhartha Gautama, the Buddha." You now know exactly what just happened to you. Without them even saying a word, you were just bathed in the consciousness of two people who were one with the Absolute. So yes, your level of consciousness has an effect on all who come into contact with you.

So how do you make this world a better place? You do it one person at a time, starting with yourself. Let's take a look at cities. Some cities are really bad places to be. But it's not the city itself that is bad—after all, a city is just a place; it's the stressed-out residents of that city who are making it an unhealthy place to live. Stress levels are so high that in some cities many of the residents are actually experiencing post-traumatic stress disorder (PTSD). What can be done? As one's own level of stress decreases, so does that of those around them. Not only that, but as one's consciousness expands (as a result of decreasing stress levels), so does the physical area that one identifies as their own. Similarly, as one's consciousness expands, so does the sphere of people whom one considers "family." Take, for example, a driver who is driving their car through their own neighborhood. If the driver is totally stressed-out and feeling disenfranchised, the chances that that driver may be driving recklessly, with little or no concern for the safety of those around them, is much greater than with a driver who is not stressed out and feels that he is a part of his community; a community that he views as an extension of his family, a family that he wants to nourish and protect. This same rationale holds true for something as petty as throwing trash on the ground. When someone is done drinking a soda, they don't throw the empty can on their own front yard, but they may throw it onto someone else's yard or out into the street. Why would they do this? Well, it's not their yard; not their street. But as one's consciousness grows, they begin to feel more of a connection with everything and everyone around them. There arises within them an awareness of how their actions, no matter how seemingly insignificant, affect their surroundings. They start to feel that every yard is their yard; every street is their street. They start to perceive the connection between themselves and the entire planet and all its inhabitants.

Have you ever noticed what I refer to as someone's "level of awareness?" Many people have what I would consider a low level of awareness. It can express itself in something as minor as going into a friend's backyard and not shutting the gate behind you, to walking across the room during a yoga class and stepping on someone else's yoga mat. How much effort does it take to shut the gate or to step around someone's yoga mat? It's not the effort; it's the awareness. As your consciousness grows as you move along your path to self-realization, so does your level of awareness.

There is a story of a king who was grooming his three sons to help him rule his kingdom. The king wanted to test his sons' levels of awareness, so he set up an elaborate contraption whereby if someone walked into his chamber, a pillow would fall from a hidden ledge over the doorway and onto the person walking through. The king summoned his youngest son into the room, and as he entered the pillow fell from the hidden ledge over the doorway. Just as it touched his shoulder, the young prince drew his sword and spun around, slicing the falling pillow in two. Seeing this, the king said, "Very good, my son."

The king next summoned his middle son. As this son walked into the room, the pillow started to fall, but before it could even reach him the prince drew his sword and sliced it in two. The king looked at this son and said, "My son, your reflexes are second to none."

Finally, the king summoned his eldest son into the room. As this son was passing through the doorway, he lifted his arm up over his head and pushed the pillow back onto the ledge before it could even start to fall. The king looked at the eldest prince and smiled.

As your spiritual awareness grows with your practice of meditation, you continue to perceive and enjoy all of the diversity around you, while at the same time being cognizant of the underlying unity. There is no "other"; everything feels like your own. There is also the feeling that you don't need to possess everything, as there is nothing "else" to possess. You do your work, and what comes, comes. When one sees only separation, desires spring up, and desires bring an unending cycle of happiness and sorrow. Liberation is not having all your desires met; it is freedom from desires. When you are established in the state of unity, you enjoy the apparent world of diversity while all the while remaining rooted in the awareness that there is no separation; yours is a world of peace and contentment.

These same points also apply to countries. There aren't bad countries; just countries with stressed-out rulers and citizens with their accompanying low levels of consciousness. Seeing only separation, these stressed-out people put classifications on everyone, separating them into groups based on religion, race, nationality, sex, sexual orientation, social and economic status—you name it. These individuals then identify themselves as members of one or more of these limited groups, and all those who do not fit into their self-identified classifications are deemed "others"; others to be discriminated against either by thought, action, or both. So no, you don't save a city or a country; you save their citizens—one person at a time.

There is a well-known story of a young girl who goes to the ocean after a big storm. On the beach are thousands upon thousands of sand dollars that have washed up on the shore. The girl starts picking up sand dollars and throwing them back into the sea. A man comes over to her and asks what she's doing, and she replies that she is saving the sand dollars. He tells her that she is wasting her time, as there are thousands and thousands of sand dollars and what she is doing won't make any difference. She bends over and picks up a sand dollar, and as she throws it back into the ocean she says, "Well, it makes a difference to this one!"

CHAPTER 28

Setting the Stage

The Absolute is ever-present; it is the very essence of everything. Nothing that we do can bring us any closer to it, as there is never any separation between the unchanging Ultimate Reality and its seemingly diverse universe of manifestations (of which we are a part). They are one and the same, just as water and ice, though appearing to be dissimilar with different characteristics, are both the exact same chemical compound: H_2O. If nothing we do can take us to this Ultimate Reality, take us from its relative aspect into its absolute aspect, why do any sadhana (spiritual practices) at all? Why not just sit back and wait for the Absolute to reveal itself to us? After all, isn't that exactly what must happen? The seemingly hidden, mystical Absolute must somehow just come out of the shadows and present itself to us? Well, actually, that is kind of what happens. We don't make progress by our own efforts; we just get "still" and the Self will be revealed. So what is this "stillness" that are we talking about, and how do we get it? It is the stillness that we come to embody as a result of our practices, our practices done for gaining knowledge and experience. For, you see, what we are doing when we gain knowledge and experience is setting the stage, creating the conditions for the Self, the "I" of "Who am I?" to reveal itself. When will this revelation take place? Well, it happens when it happens. And while we may get glimpses or hints of the Absolute when we meditate, these tastes of higher states of consciousness can happen at any time, both during and outside of meditation. But when the full glory of the Absolute is revealed, it doesn't come to us as a glimpse or hint or taste. It hits us like a freight train, with no question of its arrival.

So meditation can bring us to the door of the Absolute, but it can't actually take us into the Absolute? Correct. Imagine that merging with the Absolute is like entering into a lake that can only be entered via a diving board. To enter the lake, however, you can't jump off the diving board, as that requires some effort, and any effort, no matter how slight, is too much effort. So how do we get into this lake of the Absolute? What is the purpose of gaining all this knowledge and experience that we have been talking about, if it can't take us into the Absolute? The purpose is to get us onto the diving board. Once we are standing on the diving board, we no longer need any of what we have learned or gained from our pursuits of knowledge and experience, none of the wisdom that we have accumulated, as all that was only useful in getting us onto the diving board. It can't take us any further. It can't take us into the lake. So once we are standing on the diving board, how are we to get into the lake, if we can't jump off or push off in any way? What are we to do? Well, this is the easy part. All we have to do is let go. We just give up all our efforts, all our trying, and let go. Nothing else is needed. We just relax and let go and fall off into the lake. Like that, the Absolute will reveal itself, absorb us, with no effort whatsoever on our part.

So where is this lake of the Absolute? Is it in some far-off land? Not at all. It is the closest of the closest, as it is none other than our very own nature, our Self, and that of all that appears to surround us. And the diving board? Where is that diving board, that door to the Absolute? It is none other than our own heart. Not the physical organ that pumps our blood, but the spiritual heart, the pure consciousness that lies at the center of all.

So how do we set the stage? What knowledge and experience should we be gathering to take us to our goal, take us to that diving board over the lake of the Absolute? The various religions seem to be saying that they have the keys to heaven, that they alone possess the true word of God. The organizations promoting meditation profess that theirs is the best technique. Others say that knowledge is all that is needed and that they have that knowledge. It gets a little confusing.

Let's take a look at religion. Everyone who chooses to follow a religious tradition should believe that theirs is the best—for them. If they didn't think theirs was the best, they would change their religion. If a Buddhist thought that Islam was the best, he or she would switch to Islam. If a Christian thought that Judaism was the best, he or she would switch to Judaism. The problem arises when someone believes that their religion is the best *for everyone*, and they then try to convince others of their misguided belief. Misguided? Yes, misguided, for anyone who believes that any religion is the best is stuck in the relative, for in the Absolute there is no religion. There just is.

It's like religious leaders who profess that only men can be priests. Are they serious? Do they really believe that there is something called male or female in the Absolute? Do they really believe that God dictates that only male priests can lead someone to the kingdom of heaven? The problem is that these religious leaders have only their dogmas to pass on to their followers. They are not established in the Absolute, in the Ultimate Truth, and, as such, all that they have to convey is what is in their heads: Words and concepts that have been passed on to them by others; others who also were not established in the Absolute. And how do we know that these religious leaders are not established in the Absolute? We know because no one established in the Absolute would make such a ridiculous statement as that "God" dictates that only men can be priests. But these religious leaders proclaim that these dictates that they are espousing have come directly from God. Well, trust me, something has been lost along the way. *Merge* with "God," become established in the Absolute, discover the "I" of "Who am I?" and then let's see how the conversation goes.

When we first moved to Haddonfield in the early '60s, my mother was talking to our next-door neighbor across the fence in our backyard. Our neighbor was an elderly woman, and they got to talking about religion. At the end of their conversation, our new neighbor told my mom that she was sorry that my mother was going to go to hell. According to our neighbor, my mom was going to go to hell because this "Christian" woman believed that only Christians went to heaven, but not all Christians; only Christians who went to her church. Everyone else was going to hell.

You may believe that when others have knowledge of the Ultimate Truth and they then pass it on to you, you now possess that knowledge. This may seem true, but in actuality it is not the receiving of so-called knowledge that sets the stage for the Absolute to reveal itself; it is the understanding, and all understanding takes place from within. If all we have is intellectual knowledge, then all we will have is intellectual understanding, and for "knowing" the Absolute, if all we have is intellectual understanding, we really have no understanding at all. It's like having a complete understanding about pizza. If you know everything about pizza: How to make it, how to cook it, how to serve it—but you have never actually *tasted* pizza—well then, you really don't know pizza at all. The taste is the experience, is the knowing, and all experience comes from within. It is the experience of the Absolute that we seek, and as the Absolute is ever-present and is our true Self, our true nature, the "I" of "Who am I?" there is nothing we need to do in order to know it. We just need to get out of our own way. Just be "still" and let the Absolute shine through.

We are all familiar with obtaining knowledge. We do it throughout our entire lives. But what kind of knowledge are we gathering and for what purpose? We are gathering relative knowledge for use in the relative world. And what is relative knowledge? All knowledge is relative, as knowledge is of the nature of the intellect, and the intellect is rooted in the relative. The Absolute is beyond mind, beyond intellect: It just is. But if all knowledge is relative, yet we need knowledge and experience to move us along in our search for enlightenment, how can knowledge help us to realize the Absolute? What we do is we use knowledge to go beyond knowledge. We use the mind to go beyond the mind. But putting all this into words that can be comprehended is just not going to happen. But let's not let that stop us from trying. But remember: The Absolute cannot be intellectually understood, no matter how many words we use to describe it, or how many of our questions are answered.

We all gather basic knowledge as we are growing up. We learn that fire is hot, ice is cold, water is wet, etc. We go to school and we learn to read and write, do math, and obtain all kinds of knowledge to help us earn a living and make our way through life. Some of us are born with the gift of great intelligence, and we go on to become brain surgeons, rocket scientists, or theoretical astrophysicists. But no matter how much knowledge we gather as we move through life, it's all the same basic concept: We just keep learning more and more. Think of it as gaining knowledge through books. We read a book, absorb its knowledge, then put it down. We then read another book, and when we are done, we put it on top of the last book we read, accumulating a great stack of books as we make our way through life. Our pile of books gets higher and higher, but no matter how many books we read, no matter how much knowledge we gather, there is always one more book to read, one more bit of information that we can obtain and add to our pile. All this knowledge is helpful in the relative aspect of life, but no matter how much knowledge we gather, no matter how high our pile of books gets, it will never merge us into the

Absolute. And why not? Because it's not knowledge, intelligence, or cleverness that takes us into the Absolute—it's emptiness. It's a type of accumulated knowledge that diminishes daily. It's an emptiness that grows and grows until there is nothing left except total and complete silence. And what do we find in this total and complete silence, in this total and complete emptiness? We find an unbounded fullness that will never diminish. An empty "fullness" that we inherently know to be our true Self. So, while for teaching purposes it can be said that knowledge and experience is what leads us to that diving board over the lake of the Absolute, our understanding of what that knowledge and experience actually is, must, and will, evolve as we move along our chosen path.

As our spiritual knowledge grows, there may be a tendency to think that we actually know more than others. That we know something that others do not and that that somehow makes us more "advanced" than those whom we believe do not have our level of understanding. This will pass as we come to understand that there is nothing to know and no one to know it.

There is a story of two priests who lived in an ancient kingdom that was made up of many islands. While rowing their boat from one island to another, the priests were taken off course by strong currents, causing them to go by what was thought to be an uninhabited island. As they got nearer, they heard voices coming from the island. One priest turned to the other and said, "Do you hear that? There are people living on that island."

The other said, "I know. I thought the island was uninhabited."

As they passed closer, the first priest said, "Listen to that. The islanders are singing sacred chants."

The other priest said, "Isn't God great! These islanders are totally cut off from the rest of the world and yet they still worship God and sing his praises."

They continued to row past the island when the first priest said, "You know those islanders were not singing the sacred chants correctly. Do you think we should go back and instruct them as to how to sing the chants in the proper manner?"

The other said, "Absolutely! Let's go back!" So the two priests turned their boat around and rowed to the island. As they rowed up onto the beach, the villagers all ran over to greet them. These islanders were so excited. Even though none of them had ever seen a priest before, they knew right away that these men were priests, and they all bowed and showed great respect. The priests were delighted to see these very pious people and after some brief introductions, the priests told the villagers that they had heard them singing sacred chants, but that they could not help but notice that they were not singing them correctly. The villagers said they were so sorry. They did not realize that they were singing the chants incorrectly, and they humbly asked the priests if they would be so kind as to instruct them in the proper way. The priests, of course, were only too happy to instruct these newly discovered island people, and they told them exactly how to sing the chants. The villagers thanked them, and the priests got back into their boat and rowed away. As the priests rowed out, they were beaming. They were so happy to have been able to help out these villagers.

The first priest said, "Boy, this has been a great day. It felt so good to have met those villagers and helped them out with their chanting."

The second priests said, "I know. I'm glad we went back."

The first priest then said, "Me too. You know the ancient scriptures say that if you sing those chants correctly, you can walk on water."

The second priest said, "I know, I have read that also." All of a sudden they started to hear this splashing sound, and as they turned to look back toward the island, they saw all the villagers running out to them—on the water!

As the villagers got to their boat, they said, "Excuse us, dear priests, but we seem to have forgotten the correct way to sing the chants. Would you please instruct us one more time?"

CHAPTER 29

The Taste of a Banana

So we're going to meditate every day and gather as much knowledge as we can in our quest for enlightenment. Don't concern yourself with when you are going to get there; just enjoy the path. And know it to be a pathless path, for while you need perseverance, determination, and mental clarity at all times, you only need be natural, as the Self is not attained by doing anything other than remaining still and being as you are.

There's a story of three monks who were all seeking enlightenment. One day all three were together with the master when the eldest monk asked when he would become enlightened. The master told him that he wouldn't be enlightened in this lifetime, but he would be in the next. The eldest monk was quite upset and said he didn't want to wait until the next lifetime, and, dejectedly, he left the room. The next monk then asked the same question, "When will I become enlightened?"

The master said, "Not for ten lifetimes."

Hearing this, the monk said, "Ten lifetimes? How can I wait ten lifetimes?" as he sadly exited the room.

This left the youngest monk alone in the room with the master. Very timidly, he asked, "Master, will I ever become enlightened?"

The master looked at him compassionately and said, "My son, the road will be very long for you. You will not become enlightened for a hundred thousand lifetimes."

With this, the young monk jumped into the air and threw his hands up over his head as he exclaimed with jubilation, "Yes! Yes! I'm going to become enlightened!"

Again, we don't technically "become" enlightened, as that would mean that at one time we don't have it and at another we do. On top of that, those on the path to self-discovery may believe that they are persons; these individual, separate mind-body complexes who are seeking something, something that is separate and distinct from them. This is not the case. There is nothing "else" to discover. It's just that ignorance falls off and we are left with what was always there. Enlightenment is just the dropping of delusion. But how did this delusion come about?

Newborn babies do not understand that they are separate persons from their mothers. They think that they are one and the same. It is a gradual process for a baby to develop a belief of its own separate existence. Our five senses create the appearance that things are separate and distinct from each other and from us. From these sense-derived impressions (and our upbringing) we come to believe that we are each these separate and limited mind-body complexes. We create this feeling of separateness and limitation, and then seek to realize the oneness and become unlimited. All our efforts are only for giving up these false notions. Let's look at it like this: Picture a drop of water in the middle of the ocean. This drop of water is surrounded by a nonexistent, self-imagined sheath of individuality; there is nothing there, yet this drop of water believes itself to be an entity that is separate from the rest of the universe; in our example, the ocean. One day this drop of water gets the desire to search for this mystical thing called "the ocean." What does this drop of water, with its self-imposed, delusional idea that it is a separate entity have to do in order to find the ocean, to become one with the ocean? Nothing. Nothing but let go of the false, self-created belief that it is somehow separate from the ocean. And when this drop of water does this, are we left with a drop of water that now has the awareness that it is, and always was, part of the ocean? Not exactly, as now there is no drop of water; there is only what there always was—the ocean. Does that mean that the drop of water no longer exists and that it never existed? Again, not exactly. The drop of water always existed, just not as it believed it did. It now knows that it is, and always was, just a non-separate, undivided part of the ocean.

Let's imagine that the Ultimate Truth, the Ultimate Reality, is the taste of a banana. Once you have had the taste of a banana, you know your true Self. So you go out on your quest to find the taste of a banana. You come upon those who are more than willing to tell you what a banana tastes like. The problem is that not only have these people never tasted a banana, they have never even seen a banana. But you continue on your quest. You start reading books on bananas, all in an attempt to discover the taste of a banana. You go to lectures on what a banana tastes like, but still you cannot discover the taste. Through your many years of research, you develop a concept of what a banana tastes like, and you think you may know somewhat what it tastes like, but you're still not sure. Finally you meet the person you have been looking for: Someone who has actually *tasted* a banana. This person has not only tasted a banana; he eats bananas everyday for breakfast, lunch, and dinner. There's more. This person is a fifth-generation banana grower, and his family has been growing and eating bananas for over 150 years! Guess what? This person still can't give you the taste of a banana. He tries to tell you what a banana tastes like, but even though you have read hundreds of books on the subject, you still don't understand what he is saying, and really, you aren't looking for words to tell you what a banana tastes like; you are looking for the actual taste. This fellow is a kind, old gentleman, and he says, "Come with me." He takes you to a secret location at the back of his farm and points to a tree. He says, "See that tree over there? That is a banana tree. And see those yellow things hanging from it? Those are bananas. Go over there and pick one of those bananas, peel off the outside, and have a bite."

You are beside yourself. You thank him and go over and pick this beautiful, yellow banana, peel off the skin, and take a bite. Immediately you know. You have the taste of a banana. You know the Ultimate Reality and your true Self! Now what do you do with all the knowledge that you have accumulated over the years, all the books you have read, all the concepts and beliefs that you have developed about what a banana tastes like? Well, you can throw them all out the window, for what you were looking for was not intellectual knowledge, not concepts, not beliefs; what you were looking for was the taste, and you finally have it.

Leaving the farm, you come upon some friends, and they see you smiling from ear to ear. They ask what's up, and you tell them that you have just tasted a banana. They are so excited and they ask, "What did it taste like?" And like all those before you, you can't tell them. You can put it into words, but words do them no good. It's not the concept of what a banana tastes like (which is all that words can provide) that they need; what they need is the actual taste. All you can do is tell them what it *doesn't* taste like.

Neti neti (not this, not this) is a Sanskrit expression that translates to "Neither this, nor that." It is used to help understand the nature of the Absolute by first understanding what it is not. But like all intellectual undertakings regarding the Absolute, the Ultimate Reality, it doesn't quite do the trick. You see this as you go back and forth with your friends, trying to convey to them what a banana tastes like. They ask if it tastes like a carrot or an orange or a piece of ham, and you tell them no. They ask, "Does it taste like a grape, a hot dog, a turnip, watermelon, or salami?"

You tell them, "No, it doesn't taste like any of those things."

Finally, they say, "We've got it! It tastes like chicken; after all, doesn't everything taste like chicken?"

You say, "No, it doesn't taste like chicken."

They ask, "Then what does it taste like?"

And all you can say is, "Well, it tastes like a banana!" You see the difficulty. But if you were to put it into words and tell someone *who has already tasted a banana* what a banana tastes like, all you would have to do is say the word "banana" and they would know exactly what you're talking about. Question: "What does that ice cream over there taste like?" Answer: "Oh, that ice cream? That's banana ice cream."

While scripture can help us in our quest to realize the Ultimate Truth, scripture is *not* the Ultimate Truth. Words only create thoughts, mental concepts, and we must go beyond thought, beyond mind, and transcend into the Absolute. So if you believe that the Ultimate Truth is actually contained in scripture, you may want to think again. Jesus didn't *speak* the Ultimate Truth, as words can be misunderstood or interpreted differently by different people, depending upon their experience and intellect. That is why Jesus spoke in parables. We tend to be looking for intellectual answers to something that the intellect can't comprehend.

When dealing with the Absolute, words are incapable of forming a pure and untainted statement. The purest truth can only be expressed by complete silence. No, Jesus did not speak the Ultimate Truth, nor did Buddha or Krishna. They were, and are, the Ultimate Truth, as is everything in the universe, including you and me. But if everyone and everything is the Ultimate Truth, what made Jesus, Buddha, and Krishna so special? Think about it. What made them so special? It was the fact that they KNEW that they, and everything else, were the Ultimate Truth. But their *knowing* was not an intellectual one, although that was a part of it. It was something quite different. What was it? That's what your quest is about. It's something that no one can tell you, something that no one can give you; it is something you must realize for yourself.

Let's say that you and I go to hear a lecture given by Edward Teller, the Hungarian-American theoretical physicist colloquially known as "the father of the hydrogen bomb." His topic is on the applications of the Monte-Carlo method to statistical mechanics. Sitting next to us is Albert Einstein. All three of us listen to the lecture, and when it's over Einstein leans over and asks us how we liked it. We tell him we thought it was great. He then asks what part we liked best. We both look at him dumbfounded, for, in actuality, we didn't have a clue as to what Dr. Teller just said. Why not? Didn't we just hear the same lecture as Einstein? Well, yes and no. The words that we heard were the same, but our understanding of those words was totally different. We do not have the intellectual understanding, the experience, to know what Dr. Teller was talking about, whereas Einstein understood every word as clear as day.

Do you see how maybe, just maybe, the words in the Bible that are attributed to Jesus might not be exactly what he said? How could this be possible? While everyone who was listening to Jesus speak was *hearing* the same spoken words, each was *understanding* those words at their own level of comprehension. And as those who heard Jesus speak passed on what they heard to others, they did so from their own limited level of understanding. When Jesus' words were finally put into the Bible over 300 years after his crucifixion, those words had already been passed down many times, with each passing subject to the understandings of all those involved, including the understandings of those scribes who made the copies that were relied upon by the church. And as Jesus' words were translated over time into different languages, those translators chose words that they believed most correctly conveyed what Jesus was saying *according to their own limited levels of understanding.*

Even as to Jesus' words that were correctly recorded, do you see how someone without the necessary wisdom to understand those words might be misinterpreting what Jesus was actually trying to convey? While Jesus was speaking from his level of consciousness, a consciousness established in the Absolute, Ultimate Reality (which he described as being one with his "Father"), those hearing his words heard and understood them from their own levels of intellect, intellects rooted in the relative. This was, however, only with regard to Jesus' spoken word. As to his unspoken word, his grace that radiated out from his silent stillness, this penetrated directly into the hearts of all who were open to receiving it.

CHAPTER 30

The Clump of Dirt

We have been saying that you can't "find" the Absolute Reality, as that implies that it was somehow lost. The Vedas (ancient Hindu scriptures) say that with the removal of ignorance, the Absolute Reality is revealed. The Christian mystics described it as forgetfulness, and stated that all we need do is remember that which was never lost or separate. But if we can't *become* enlightened, as we already are, how can our just *knowing* it or our *remembering* it be all that different from our not knowing or not remembering it?

Let's look at it through this story. Once upon a time, in a far-off land, there lived a very poor farmer. His only possession was a clump of dirt attached to an old leather cord that he wore around his neck. This item had been in his family for many, many generations, and had been passed on to him by his father. For some long-forgotten reason, this clump of dirt was supposedly very important, and the man's father had told him that he should take very good care of it and protect it at all times. Being a good son, this man did as his father asked and he took very good care of his clump of dirt, making sure to not let anything happen to it.

One day the farmer was crossing a small river after a heavy rainfall. Due to the recent downpour, the river was flowing much more strongly than usual, and as he was crossing the farmer lost his footing and fell into the water, being quickly swept downstream by the current. Fortunately, he was eventually able to swim to the bank and pull himself out. But then he remembered: The clump of dirt! He looked down and it was gone. The water had washed it away. But there, in its place, was a diamond. Not just any diamond, but the largest, most perfect diamond the world had ever known, making him rich beyond his wildest dreams. What happened was that over the generations, the diamond had become covered by dirt, and since his ancestors could no longer see it, they had forgotten that it was there. They knew that there was something of value attached to the cord; they just could not remember what. Now when did this man become rich? He didn't become rich—he was *always* rich; he just didn't know it. But now he knows.

Since the farmer was always rich, did that mean that by his simply knowing it his life wouldn't change that much? Hardly. His life changed tremendously, as he could now provide for his family, and they would never feel the pains of poverty again. For, you see, there is a big, big difference between being rich and not knowing it, and being rich AND knowing it. The difference is like being stuck out in the desert with no water and knowing that by drinking a big glass of water your life will saved, and actually obtaining and *drinking* a big glass of water.

By analogy, this is somewhat like what happens with self-realization. The difference between intellectually knowing that you are not the body or mind, but instead Pure Consciousness, and KNOWING that you are not the body or mind, but Pure Consciousness, is like night and day. It's like knowing without KNOWING and knowing with "KNOWING." When the farmer became aware of his diamond, his life changed forever. On the outside, all the material needs of his family were met. On the inside, all his money-related worries left him forever. With the enlightened person, the change is not on the "outside"; it is on the "inside," and while this may or may not have an effect on his or her apparent outside actions, it most definitely affects how he or she perceives and understands the world around him or her. He or she can still see and interact appropriately with all the apparent diversity that surrounds him or her, all the while "KNOWING" that all this seeming diversity is but an apparent manifestation of his or her own being. All is merely the Absolute interacting with the Absolute; God's divine play, or "Lila," if you will. For you see, the world that the ignorant perceive is not as it appears; the world in the eyes of the enlightened is indescribable. There is no spoon!

While it's fun to intellectualize about the Absolute and self-realization, it's a world of difference from actually living it. Talking about spirituality with others can sometimes end up being just a bunch of head trips: My guru is a satguru (true teacher) and he's better than that guru. Or: The philosophy of non-duality (Advaita) is the correct one and not that of duality. Or: My God is the only true God. Or how about this one: This book of scripture is sacred, and you can't take it with you when you go into the restroom because that would somehow be sacrilegious. Seriously? So you're telling me that a temple's altar is a holier place than a bathroom stall. That God is more present in a church, temple, or mosque than in an outhouse. Really? Interesting. You need to be established in the Absolute to reap the benefits of its full glory and unbounded joy. You need the taste of the banana. The talk is just talk.

The spiritual masters of the past (Krishna, Buddha, and Jesus, to name a few) were all self-realized, all having discovered the "I" of "Who am I?" They did not want their followers to worship them: They wanted them to realize the same Ultimate Truth that they themselves had discovered. They passed on to these followers the knowledge of how to reach "God," but over time those paths of self-discovery that they laid out have been lost, being replaced by dogma and hollow ritual, leaving us, unfortunately, with the blind leading the blind.

CHAPTER 31

A World of Sand

How did all this apparent confusion about what is real or unreal come about? We look around and see infinite diversity, and we see that we are separate and distinct from everyone and everything. Are we really to believe that who or what we truly are is exactly the same as every other human being on the planet? Are we to believe that we are the same as a squirrel, a tree, a rock, or even some far-off, distant star? Are we to believe that we were never born and will never die, as we are somehow some mystical force, some absolute, all-pervading, eternal consciousness? Well, first of all, we aren't to believe anything. We aren't looking for some fact to believe in. It's not information that we seek; it's knowledge. We are looking for the Ultimate Truth, the taste of the banana. And while we must start our search in the relative, using our minds and intellects as our instruments of discovery, at some point we will come to understand that while everything in the relative is but a manifestation of the Ultimate Truth, our realization of this does not happen in the relative; it happens in the Absolute. And as our minds and intellects are grounded in the relative, they cannot take us into the Absolute. At some point we must go beyond mind and intellect and just be.

Trying to look at this intellectually, the universe and everything in it came from some mysterious, unknown source, and everything is only that from which it sprang. Exactly what was (is) this source that created the universe? When humans see something for the first time, or have some type of new concept, we put a name to it, a label. Why do we do this? One reason is for communication. For example: What is an apple? Well, an apple is an apple. It is this thing that English-speaking people call "apple," Spanish-speaking people call "manzana," and French-speaking people call "pomme." An apple is this thing that has different names, depending on what language you are using.

Some people call the source of the universe "God," a word that has different meanings to different people. Some believe that God is a being that sits on a throne somewhere, maybe up in the clouds. Others believe that God is some kind of energy or force, while others believe that there is no such thing as God. But really, "God" is a word that represents some unseen being or thing, which may or may not exist, depending on who you are talking to. Why is it that when we say "apple" (or "manzana" or "pomme"), everyone is thinking about the same thing, and no one denies its existence? It's because an apple belongs to the relative, and everyone with functioning senses can perceive it and know and understand what it is. This being or thing that we refer to as "God," however, belongs to the Absolute, and our senses don't perceive the Absolute. Not that the Absolute can't be known—it can; just not as most people would understand. To *know* the Absolute is to *be* the Absolute.

The Bible says that God created the universe when he spoke, saying: Let there be light, let there be firmament, let there be water, and so forth. It was the "word" of God, the vibration of his voice, which brought the universe into existence. Since I assume that nothing existed before this universe was created, except this thing called "God," I must assume that the universe was created out of God. It was God creating this universe out of his own being. So according to Christianity and Judaism, we can say that the source of the universe is this thing called "God."

According to Hindu scriptures, the universe was created by Brahman (the Ultimate Reality) with the sacred sound of Om (Aum). It was the vibration of the sound "Om" that brought the universe into existence. Actually, Hindu scriptures say that the universe is Brahman, this ever-existing reality, and, as such, the universe was not created at all. It's just a big cycle of Brahman solely in its unmanifested, absolute nature, and Brahman in its unmanifested, absolute nature, *together* with its manifested, relative nature. So according to Hinduism, we can say that the source of the universe is this thing called "Brahman."

The prevailing scientific belief is that the universe was created some 13.8 billion years ago by what is called the Big Bang theory. Science believes that nothing existed prior to the creation of the universe except for a minuscule point of matter, smaller than the size of an electron. Actually, an electron has no discernable size; so really, we can view this point of "matter" as nonexistent. There was some type of expansion, or stretching, of this minuscule point of matter, and within a tiny fraction of a second the universe came into existence as light and energy. This light and energy then evolved into the universe as we know it today. So according to science, we can say that the source of the universe is this thing, referred to as "an infinitesimally small point of matter," which almost instantly expanded and stretched out to create the basis of what has evolved into this universe, as we know it.

So really, how did this universe come into existence? First, Einstein has stated that the universe is incomprehensible, but let's not let that get in our way. You don't get something out of nothing, so even if nothing physically existed (nothing of any mass) immediately prior to the creation of the universe, something existed. And, like the first person to encounter an apple, we can put any name we want to this "nothingness" from which, or by which, this universe came into existence. We can call it God or Brahman or a nonexistent point of matter. We could also call it the Absolute, Pure Consciousness, or the Ultimate Truth. What we name it is really not important; it is what it is. So, now, going back to my conversation with minister Dan outside the Y in Charleston, is everything in the universe truly what it appears to be in its individual, physical form, or is it really what it was before this universe came into existence? You tell me. All that exists in the universe existed before anything existed, before the universe was created. It existed in its seed form, just as an ice-sculptured swan exists in the block of ice before the sculptor carves it out. And just as the carved swan's true nature is ice, the true nature of the universe, and everything in it, is that which it was before there was anything. So if we are looking to discover our true nature, we don't have to look far, for we already are our true nature; we have just forgotten what it is.

Let's look at it like this: Imagine that the ultimate building block of the entire physical universe, this thing that we have been calling the *Ultimate Truth*, *Pure Consciousness*, or the *Absolute*, is sand. Sand is all that exists, and everything is made only of sand. (Actually, before the discovery of the atom, people thought that grains of sand were the building blocks of everything that they saw around them). Picture it as an endless expanse of sand. This sand suddenly takes on various and diverse forms and shapes, not unlike what happens at the beach on a sunny summer day when children build their sand castles. So now instead of just this expanse of flat sand, some of the sand has taken on the appearance of houses and trees and turtles and fish and people of every shape and size. Let's give some of these creations the ability to move around, and make them conscious.

So now we have all these things made of sand, including sentient sand people. Question: When were these sand people created? When did they come into existence? Well, really, they were never created and never came into existence, for while they may all appear to exist, and they may believe that they exist, they are actually nothing but sand. None of these creations have any existence at all apart from the sand that has taken on their apparent forms. And while all these "creations" are in a constant state of change, the sand itself is always changeless. It has undergone no change whatsoever.

As these sand people are sentient, they have taken on a sense of existence and self. They have become the "knowers," and all that surrounds them has become the "known." They have even become the knowers of themselves. But have they? Do they really know the true nature of themselves and that of all that surrounds them? They know their thoughts and emotions, and they can see themselves in the mirror, but do they really know who they are? Their senses perceive everything around them. But is all as it appears? No. It is all a mirage. The true nature of themselves and that of all that surrounds them, what they and everything else are, and have always been, and will always be, is pure sand. But why would they know this? They wouldn't, because to the sand people the sand is not known, as none of their senses can perceive it. Likewise, none of our senses can perceive that we, and everything else in our universe, are nothing but the apparent manifestations of the unknowable underlying Pure Consciousness, the Absolute.

But there were rumors swirling around the world of the sand people. Legend had it that long ago a very special sand person had discovered his true nature: That being that he, and everyone and everything, were not these individual separate creations that seemed to be coming in and out of existence, seemed to be being born only to later meet this event called "death," but rather everyone and everything was actually this ever-present, ever-existent thing called "sand." Now most of the sand people thought that this was just crazy talk, but a few, a very few, believed this legend and they started on a quest to discover their true nature, to discover this thing called "sand." Now here

215

are some questions for the day: What do these seekers of the truth have to do in order to know that they are sand? What do they have to do to become sand? And where do they have to go to make these discoveries? Well, they don't have to *do* anything or *go* anywhere. They are, and always will be, sand, and nothing they do will bring about what already is. All they need to do is: "Be still and know that they are sand."

CHAPTER 32

Religion

Why is it that we sometimes hear media accounts of members of the ministry abusing children, misappropriating funds, or acting in other inappropriate ways? Or how about clerics who, in the name of God, go about spewing discrimination and hatred of others? How is this possible? After all, aren't these people servants of God? (You know: Do unto others, as you would have others do unto you; love thy neighbor as thyself; judge not that ye be not judged). As I see it, very few members of the clergy have any direct experience of the concepts they preach. Most have only misguided, intellectual understandings of the religious positions that they are promoting and just regurgitate things that they have read or heard from others. If these religious leaders had the actual experience of higher states of consciousness—the levels of consciousness of the Jesuses, Krishnas, and Buddhas of the world—to complement their intellectual knowledge, the commission of these questionable acts would be highly improbable, if not impossible. But where does this experience of these higher states of consciousness come from? It comes from going within ("For behold, the kingdom of God is within you"), and it is something espoused by all religions. It is found in the Sufism of Islam, the Kabbalah of Judaism, the meditations of Hinduism, Buddhism, and Jainism, and the mystics of Christianity. Unfortunately, these practices of going within to gain the experience of the respective foundational religious tenets have been left out by so many of the religious leaders of today.

Enlightened masters speak, not by rotely repeating the historical scriptures of their religious traditions, but rather by relating their *own* experiences in terms of their historical scriptures. But they do not stop there. The masters speak in terms of all scripture, regardless of artificial, man-made religious divides, as they are living the one truth that is expressed in so many different ways by all the religions of the world. Think of it as if asking a Frenchman, who has the limited language skills of only being able to speak French, to describe a sunset. He'll describe it in French, not Chinese. But if you were to ask a Frenchman, who has the linguistic skills to speak every language, to describe a sunset, he could do so in any and all languages.

When Jesus said, "I am the way, and the truth, and the life. No one comes to the Father except through me," he was speaking from his own experience, the one universal truth. That truth is "I." "I" am the way. "I" am the truth. "I" am the life. But who is this "I" that Jesus spoke of? Was it the "I" of the person Jesus, the physical man who walked the earth 2,000 years ago or was it a different "I"? Search for yourself with the question: "Who am I?" Find for yourself this "I" of "Who am I?" and you'll discover not only your own "I," but also the "I" that Jesus spoke of. Take

your quest to the end and you'll find yourself at the beginning, for that "I," the Ultimate Truth, isn't something
separate and distinct. There are not two "I"s; one to search
and the other to be found. There is only one. It is the "I"
of "I am what I am" that was spoken to Moses on Mount
Horeb over 3,300 years ago.

So, do we need to abandon religion, as John
Lennon suggested in his song "Imagine," in order for all
the people to live in peace? No. What we need is for those
who do choose to follow religious traditions to go deeper
into their religions, beyond the questionable dogmas that
have sprung up from humankind's limited understanding
of their "divine" scriptures; scriptures that, although possibly divinely inspired, have nevertheless been recorded
and passed down through the ages by those who lacked
the higher states of consciousness necessary to understand and relate these esoteric messages to others.

How could "scripture" be questionable? Let's reit-
erate, using the New Testament of the Bible once again as
our example. The New Testament of the Bible was codified
by the Catholic church in the fourth century, using writings from the first and second century by people who had
never met Jesus who used accounts of others who had also
never met Jesus. As there were no printing presses at the
time, these early writings were copied by scribes who were
barely literate and thus subject to mistakes and changes.
Added to this, as these copies were translated from one
language into another, they were subject to the limited understandings of the translators who chose the words that
they believed most correctly conveyed the meanings of the
writings that they were translating.

The four gospels chosen for inclusion in the New Testament, Matthew, Mark, Luke, and John, more or less put the people on a lower rung, God on a higher rung, and the church in the middle. To get to God you had to go through the church. They had the keys to heaven. Be faithful to the church, worship God as they dictated, and your reward would be an eternity in heaven at God's side. Disagreeing with the church's dictates, such as the sun revolving around the Earth, was to risk being labeled a heretic, or worse yet, being burned alive at the stake.

Why did the church choose these four gospels for the New Testament and none of the other fifty-four or so Gnostic gospels that were circulating at the time? Gospels that not only did the church not want included in the Bible, but gospels that the church wanted destroyed? Could it be that the church had an ulterior motive? Was it that the Gnostics viewed Jesus not as someone placed on earth to be worshiped, but rather as someone who had somehow merged with God and who could guide others to also know and merge with God? Was it that the Gnostics did not need an organized church to reach God, as their path was based more on their personal relationship with God? The reality is that there is no *merging* with anything, as there is no "other." There aren't two things that need to be merged; there just "is"; just the "I am" and its understanding; understanding that you will never get from any outside source. This is not to say that outside sources can't be helpful on the spiritual path, they are very helpful, but at some point they must all be let go of and dropped, as all that you believe to be external and separate is not that at all; it is just a projection that we have come to believe as a reality. So yes, knowledge and experience, the mind and the intellect, are the tools needed to move our awareness and understanding toward the Ultimate Truth, but to enter its kingdom, these tools must all be left at the door.

Why did the Catholic church tell my mother's generation and my grandmother's generation that they should not read the Bible, saying that to do so would only *confuse* them? Why were they told that only the priests should read the Bible and that they in turn would explain its meanings to them? What was in this church-codified Bible that parishioners wouldn't understand or would somehow misunderstand? If you look closely, the New Testament is both a directive and guide, albeit very esoteric and somewhat incomplete, to search inward to find and know God. Here are just a few of the more obvious, relevant passages:

"The light of the body is the eye: therefore when thine eye is single the whole body is full of light . . . If thy whole body therefore be full of light, having no part dark, the whole shall be full of light . . ." (Luke 11:34–36).

"The kingdom of God cometh not with observation: Neither shall they say, Lo here! Or lo there! For behold, the kingdom of God is within you." (Luke 17:20–21).

"But thou, when thou prayest, enter into thy closet, and when thou hast shut thy door, pray to thy Father which is in secret; and thy Father which seeth in secret shall reward thee openly." (Matthew 6:6.)

"The disciple is not above his master: but every one that is perfect *shall be* as his master." (Luke 6:40) [emphasis added].

Did Jesus teach his disciples methods to look inward (meditate) that he did not give to the crowds in general? When Jesus' disciples asked him why he spoke to the crowds in parables, he answered, "Because it is given unto you to know the mysteries of the kingdom of heaven, but to them it is not given. . . . Therefore speak I to them in parables: because they seeing see not; and hearing they hear not, neither do they understand. . . . For verily I say unto you, That many prophets and righteous men have desired to see those things which ye see, and have not seen them; and to hear those things which ye hear, and have not heard them" (Matthew 13:11–17). Obviously, those "things" that Jesus spoke of his disciples seeing and hearing were not outward things that could be perceived by the senses of the eyes and ears, otherwise those "things" could have been presented to anyone to see and hear. Those "things" that were known to the disciples came as the result of their going inward to that kingdom of God that lies within.

So no, we do not need to abandon religion to move forward (nor do we need any religion at all, if that is not our inclination); we just need to look more deeply into our religion (if we have one) to find some method to obtain the inner aspect of experience to go along with the outer aspect of knowledge. While all religions speak of this inner place, not all provide a readily available means to experience it. If you have difficulty finding a meditation technique within your own religion, then look elsewhere. Meditation is not religious by nature; it is merely a technique to settle the mind and go inward to the seat of thought and beyond. If you are sitting there thinking about things, trying to gain some intellectual understanding, then you are not meditating—you are contemplating. Contemplation has its place, just not during meditation. During meditation you are not trying to do anything, not trying to learn anything, not trying to gain anything—not an experience, not knowledge, not understanding—nothing. You are just sitting there, letting go, using some method to relax your mind and naturally and effortlessly drift inward.

If you wanted to be the best cook in the world, would you only study French cooking? If you did, I would argue that you don't want to be the best cook in the world; you only want to be the best *French* cook in the world. If you really wanted to be the best cook in the world, to know all you could about cooking, you would study every cooking method available so that you could gain all the knowledge possible on the subject. The same holds true for spiritual pursuits in the search for God/truth. To say that you want to find the ultimate God/spirituality/truth, but that you are only going to study, say, Judaism, means that you are not really looking for the Ultimate Truth; you are just looking for the ultimate *Jewish* truth. To then argue that the Ultimate Truth can only be found in Judaism is to start your journey with your cup full, something you never want to do in spiritual pursuits. You need to start with an empty cup, and continually keep emptying your cup so that you are ready and able to receive all that comes your way. You need to be able to look to all religions and spiritual traditions, to gather as much knowledge as you can, and then let go.

It's human nature to have beliefs and concepts about all kinds of stuff, but in our search for truth, we must not hold firmly to any belief or concept. We must be easy with everything that comes and just let things unfold in an effortless, natural way. So drop your fears, as you must be fearless in your pursuit. Unfortunately, so many religions have placed the fear of God as an obstacle to those advancing on the spiritual path, saying that anyone who speaks other than their limited dogmas speaks for the devil, and to even hear their voice is to condemn one to hell. Please— give me a break.

For those who have no religious affiliations, and even those who do not believe in religion or God, the same holds true—do not be afraid. If you have an interest in discovering the Ultimate Truth, you must be able to look everywhere, use every source available, for even though you will not find the Ultimate Truth in any religious scripture or esoterical spiritual writing, all may be of use in moving you along on your quest.

At first it may seem that the various religious and spiritual scriptures are all saying different, even contradictory things. But as your experience and knowledge grows, as your wisdom grows, you will see that they are all attempting to say the same thing, just at a much deeper level of understanding than what may appear on the surface. For, you see, there is not a different Ultimate Truth for each religion. There is only one Ultimate Truth. A truth that has been expressed in various ways by the enlightened masters of each religion, and misunderstood and wrongly passed on by so many that followed. Just remember: The Ultimate Truth can only be realized by you alone on your inner journey. You won't find it in a book, and no one can tell you what it is or give it to you, as it is nothing separate from you to somehow be searched for and obtained.

At some point though, we must leave religion behind, go beyond religion, for while religion *talks* about the

Ultimate Truth, it is *not* the Ultimate Truth, and it cannot take us there. It can only give us a hint of the Ultimate Truth, for religion, as do all forms of knowledge, belongs to the realm of the relative, and we need to move beyond the relative and into the realm of the Absolute. Jesus said, "Render therefore unto Caesar the things which are Caesar's; and unto God the things that are God's." While this quote from the Bible (Matthew 22:21) is widely regarded as dealing with the relationship between Christianity, government, and society, at a much deeper level of understanding it can be regarded as the relationship between the relative, which includes Christianity and all forms of religion, and the Absolute, which is beyond even the concept of God, unless you are using the word "God" as a term for the indescribable Absolute, and not for some all-powerful, all-knowing, deity.

And just as there are not separate Ultimate Truths for the various religions, there is also not a separate, scientific Ultimate Truth. If science and religion seem to profess different truths, it is only due to limited understanding on their respective parts. As scientific theories and capabilities evolve, and spiritual understandings unfold, both must eventually lead to the same truth: A truth that never came into existence, never changes, and will never cease to be. So in your quest for truth, it is not necessary, or advisable, to leave science out of the equation.

Let me tell you a story about the Ultimate Truth as it relates to my plasterer. When Niki and I moved back to New Jersey in the early '90s, we bought a big old house that was built in 1885. The house needed a total restoration, including repair of its plaster walls, which were over 100 years old. It takes a real expert to repair plaster walls properly, so we did some research and found someone whom we thought would do a good job: George Hamburger. George, who was in his eighties, had worked as a plasterer for his entire adult life, and had done a lot of plaster repair for historic restorations in the South Jersey/Philadelphia area. Niki took down all the old wallpaper in the house to get ready for the plasterer. George came over to start working and pointed out something on a newly bared wall of our foyer. It seems that back in the day, when houses were being built, plasterers would sign one of their plaster walls when they were finished with the job. Here on one of the walls of our foyer was the signature of the person who had constructed the plaster walls of our house when it was built back in 1885. It was George Hamburger's grandfather's signature! Yes, George was the best. He had it in his blood. Not only did he do a good job; he did a fantastic job.

A couple of years after George finished our plasterwork, I was talking to my friend Marcy, who had just bought a house down the street. Marcy was fixing up her house, and I told her that if she needed a plasterer, I had a great one. She said that was okay; she had already hired someone, and he was the best. I told her I didn't think so, and we went back and forth arguing over whose plasterer was the best. I knew my plasterer was the best and that whomever Marcy had could not be as good as George. But then I picked up on something from Marcy's argument. Marcy didn't just *think* her plasterer was the best: She *knew* it. Right then and there, I knew what was going on. I asked her, "Marcy, who's your plasterer?"

Her reply: "George Hamburger." So yes, while the various religions may believe that they are worshiping and passing on the teachings of different "Gods," there is only one Ultimate Reality, and it is the same for everyone.

Most religions were founded on the teachings of enlightened masters from the past; enlightened masters who tried to convey that they were somehow one with, and an integral part of, God. Since these enlightened masters were different people, the various religions that have sprung up from their teachings believe that their "Gods" are different beings, beings all decreed to be the only true God. On the physical level, the relative level, these masters were of course different people, speaking different languages and coming from different cultures and traditions. On the Absolute level, the level of Pure Consciousness, they are all the same: That one, Absolute nothingness which is the basis of, and not separate from, the entire physical universe, these enlightened masters, and, yes, you and me. When these enlightened masters spoke of themselves, others mistakenly believed that they were speaking of their individual, physical beings, the persons uttering the words. The enlightened masters knew that their physical aspects: Their bodies, minds, and thoughts, were just things that come and go, like old clothing to be discarded. Who they were, however, who or what they realized and understood themselves to be, was the underlying consciousness, the all-pervading, attributeless Being that never comes or goes, was never born, and, as such, will never die; the stuff which is manifested as the entire universe and beyond, including, of course, their individual bodies who were attempting to expound the inexpoundable.

Buddha was not a Buddhist, Jesus was not a Christian, and Muhammad was not a Muslim. They were teachers. So yes, while all the various religions may be declaring that their religion is the best, and that they are spreading the only true word of God, dig a little deeper. They are all trying, in their own limited ways, to preach the word of the one Ultimate Truth, a truth that cannot be expressed in words, not even by those who are living it. And clearly, if even the enlightened masters (the Christs, Krishnas, and Buddhas of the world) could not convey in words the Ultimate Reality, a reality that they were all living, how can religious leaders, leaders who have never had the experience of the Ultimate Truth, never "merged" and become one with the Absolute, ever believe that they are somehow conveying that truth, showing the way to that truth to their followers? Again, this is the proverbial "blind leading the blind."

Now I am in no way trying to instill any beliefs in anyone, especially beliefs of a religious or philosophical nature, but for those of you who are ready to get on the spiritual path of self-discovery, you must have faith that something else exists beyond this relative world of perception. If you are sincere in seeking the Absolute, in investigating the question "Who am I?" the first and foremost thing is to make a continuous, honest attempt to establish the conviction that the world that you see is not outside of you. As your experience grows, your conviction will strengthen. As to any beliefs that may arise as you move forward in your investigation: Don't hold onto them, as all beliefs will eventually fade into the void of knowing.

CHAPTER 33

Perception of Reality

So where are we? There is nothing to know and no one to know it. What we are dealing with is beyond the ken of any of our senses and can't even be contemplated, much less known. It just is. You don't become it: You are it. It doesn't come into your life: It is life. And you don't discover it, as it was never lost. When we talk about this Ultimate Reality, this Ultimate Truth, in this way, it all seems like just a bunch of esoteric mumbo jumbo. While all the religions, spiritual sects, and New Age soothsayers are ready and willing to tell you all about the Ultimate Truth and guide you to it: Beware. If they can tell you, and you can understand, while it may be *about* the Ultimate Truth, it's *not* the Ultimate Truth. You can't perceive, and you can't know, the Ultimate Truth, the Ultimate Reality, or what some may call "God." Why not? Because there is no you, or at least no you in the sense that most of us perceive ourselves to be. This brings us back to what we are really trying to know—the answer to the question: "Who am I?"

How do we know or perceive anything? We do it with our minds. If the mind is not working, there is no perception. If you are sitting quietly with total focus and attention on something, say studying for a test, and someone casually comes by and asks you a question, you may not respond. The person may then raise their voice and almost yell at you to get your attention. When they finally do, you may say, "Oh, I'm sorry. What did you say? I didn't hear you." Did you really not hear them the first time? Were your ears not working? No, you were just not listening, as your mind, which does the listening, was not connected to and was not receptive of what your ears were picking up.

The mind knows by what it perceives through the senses, including what it learns from others. It can then use this acquired information to contemplate and/or extrapolate additional knowledge. The entire system of the mind gaining and understanding knowledge is based on differences, on opposites. If there is no opposite value, no contrast, the mind cannot perceive nor have any concept of the matter. For example, we only have the concept of *good* by having its opposite concept of *bad*. We can only know what happiness is by having experienced sadness. There is no "big" without "small."

Let's look at the concept of temperature. We only know "hot" by experiencing and knowing "cold." Without *cold* there is no *hot*. Let's examine this a little deeper. Forgetting physics and thermodynamics for the moment, let's imagine that everything in the universe is the same "temperature"; let's say 98.6 degrees Fahrenheit. Okay, now everything is 98.6 degrees—your body, the Earth, water, ice, fire, space, the sun—everything. If that were the case, you would not, and could not, have any understanding of temperature. The concept could not even exist. If someone were to use the word "hot" and say, for example, that it was "hot" out, you would look at them as if they were half-crazy and ask, "What are you talking about? What does 'hot' mean?"

Let's take another example. Let's say I put a dozen cans of paint, all different colors, in front of you, and I ask you to pick a color and paint a wall. You look at the paint and pick out a color, let's say purple, and you paint the wall. I then say paint a picture on the wall that you just painted purple using any or all of the remaining eleven colors. You pick out a few colors and paint a picture. Could I then see the picture that you just painted? Yes. I could see your picture. Now let's say that you pick out any one of the twelve colors and you paint another wall with it. I then say paint a picture on this new wall that you just painted, using only the color that you just used to paint it with. You do as I ask and paint a picture using the same color that you just painted the wall with. Could I then see your picture? Could my mind perceive what you just painted? No. Why not? Because there is no contrast; there are no differences for my eyes to perceive. Does that mean that there is no picture painted on the wall? Not at all. There is a picture on the wall; I just can't perceive it.

So how does all this relate to our not being able to know the Ultimate Reality? Well, this Ultimate Reality, this Truth, or whatever label you want to put on it, has no characteristics, no attributes, nothing to distinguish it from anything else. Even though it is everywhere and has always existed, it just cannot be perceived, and, as such, it can't be understood or known, as there is nothing to understand or know. Does that mean that it doesn't exist? Oh, it exists all right. It's the only thing that truly does exist. All that we believe to exist—this Earth, the universe, even ourselves—is only the apparent, perceivable manifestation of this Ultimate Reality. And while everything appears to be coming and going, constantly changing with infinite variations, this is only what our minds perceive, what our senses pick up, what we have been taught to believe. This Ultimate Reality is the matrix, the essence of what everything actually is. It takes on, so to speak, the characteristics of what is being perceived, while all the while remaining unknown and unchanging, just as it is. All that appears to exist is actually just the Self *masquerading* as the manifest universe. It is like a dream. Are all the things and events that take place in a dream true? Of course not. They are just the imaginary creations of the dreamer; just the dreamer masquerading as all the people, objects, and events in his self-made dream world.

Even though there is only one reality, it can be viewed as having two aspects—the universe that we perceive (which is actually the Ultimate Reality manifesting itself as infinite diversity), and the Ultimate Reality in its unchanging, unmanifested aspect. To make our undertaking to uncover the Ultimate Reality even more problematic, we *are* simply the Ultimate Reality, a reality that has manifested as what we believe to be our own, individual selves, and as long as we believe ourselves to be these individual "persons" looking for this separate "Ultimate Reality," our search will be an endless one. It's like a fish swimming in the middle of the ocean looking for the ocean. What does the fish have to do to find the ocean?

Nothing. It just has to "know" that it is in the ocean. When it does, will it feel any different? Not at all. It will just act in harmony with its surroundings, having remembered this forgotten knowledge.

Let's take another example. What does water, and by that I mean pure, distilled water, taste like? Well, it has no taste. What if I were to stir in some sugar; now how does it taste? It tastes sweet. Now what if instead of sugar, I stir in some lemon juice. How does it taste? It now has a sour taste. Has the water changed? No. It has just taken on the taste of the sugar or lemon juice that was mixed into it, the characteristics of the sugar or lemon juice. The Ultimate Reality is like that, only there are not two separate things coming together. There is only the Ultimate Reality and the Ultimate Reality in its apparent, manifested form: Two seemingly different things that are actually only one. The Ultimate Reality, the Ultimate Truth if you will, is changeless regardless of whether we contemplate it in its unmanifested, unchanging nature, or in its apparent, manifested nature of taking on the appearance of the ever-changing universe.

So what does all this mean? It doesn't mean anything, as these are just words that are creating mental concepts, and what we are interested in is the Ultimate Truth, which is beyond concept. You need to settle your mind so that the Ultimate Truth, in its seemingly manifested form as your body and mind, merges, so to speak, with itself (from which it was never separate) in its unmanifested nature. And how do you do this? Well I can only speak from my own experience—you do some form or forms of meditation for experience and you gather knowledge from wherever you can—reading, contemplating, spending time with those whom you believe have experienced, or are experiencing and living, that which you seek to obtain. But, and this is important, this knowledge and experience does not take you to, nor merge you with, this Ultimate Truth, your true Self, as you were never separate from it; it just helps to set up a *still* state of mind that is receptive to what actually is. When the conditions are right, the tractor beam of the Absolute, of self-realization, just pulls you in.

So what happens as you move along your path? As you gain spiritual wisdom from your knowledge and experience, the benefits that are bestowed do not arrive in a vacuum—they spill over into your everyday life. Life becomes less burdensome and more joyful. It's not that things are changing all around you for the better, but rather, your perception of them is altered. Rough edges get smoother, confrontations lessen, and problems don't seem so insurmountable. But actually, things *do* change around you, for as you see the world, so it becomes for you. Your state of consciousness does affect your environment; the "outside" and the "inside" start to blend into a unified awareness, a unified awareness that is you.

We have said that with the cessation of thoughts, the Self will be revealed. We have also said that the Self is unknowable. How do we reconcile these seemingly contradictory statements? This question deals with the triad of knowing, and its answer lies in understanding the mystery of the trinity.

Knowing has three separate aspects: The knower, a thing to be known, and the act of knowing. Let's look at each of these parts as they relate to self-realization. First:

The *knower*. A knower is a conscious, thinking being. At the moment of realizing (*knowing*) the Self, all thoughts have stopped and the mind (the knower) has ceased to exist, leaving only awareness. This state is unlike sleep wherein the mind is in an unconscious state of void with no awareness of anything. Here there is *only* Pure Awareness. Thus at the moment of realization, we can say that there is no "knower."

Second: A *thing to be known*. The Self is not a "thing." Although it manifests as the physical universe, a universe that, at the relative level, is capable of being known, at the unmanifested level of the Absolute it has no attributes, thus we can say that there is "nothing to know."

Third: The *act of knowing*. The act of knowing is the conscious connection between two things—the knower and the thing to be known. But as there is neither a knower nor thing to be known, there can be no connection, no "act of knowing."

So where does this leave us? While the Self is not a *thing* to become aware of by some separate, nonexistent *knower*, the Self does exist, and it exists as everything, including the nonexistent knower. So in our triad of knowing the Self, there is no knower, or thing to be known, or act of knowing; there is only the ever-existent Self. Thus we say: "To *know* the Self is to *be* the Self."

After you come into contact with the Absolute, when your mind returns to its "normal" state, it brings with it a little (or a lot) of the Absolute. Again, it's like dipping a white cloth into a dye solution; every time you pull the cloth out, it has a little more of the color of the dye imparted onto it. As you come in and out of contact with the Absolute during your daily meditation practice, you (your mind) start to perceive and interact with the world, and all those in it, in a somewhat different manner. Things no longer seem so separate from one another or from you. You see and appreciate the wonders of diversity that surround you, while at the same time you feel the unity of the Absolute that underlies it all. Things are no longer as good or bad, as black or white, as you may have once perceived them to be. They just are. Where you previously saw only diversity and separation, you now start to see the oneness, the unity, of the underlying Absolute with the overlying shadows of its manifestations superimposed upon it. You start to accept people and situations as they are, putting no labels on them, taking everything as it comes. This is not to say that you just coast through life doing nothing. On the contrary, you give everything your 100 percent, only now there is no feverishness or fear in your actions. Things are happening through you, not by you. You don't take credit for any of your so-called successes, nor blame for any so-called failures. You just give your 100 percent and whatever happens, happens. You simply enjoy whatever bounty comes your way through your efforts, whether it be great or small.

Some seekers of truth have this fear that if they find this Ultimate Reality and then "merge" into it, they will then somehow forever cease to exist. They will just become an undifferentiated part of this vast, unbounded consciousness, leaving no individual thinking being behind. Fear not. It's not quite like that. It's more analogous to a caterpillar going into a cocoon and coming out the other end as a butterfly. The state of Samadhi is one where the individual mind has fully merged with its source (the Absolute) and ceases to exist as a separate, conscious, functioning organism. In this state of Unity, there is only one—the bliss of Pure Consciousness, the "I" of "I am." When one comes out of Samadhi, the mind becomes aware and can once again function in the realm of the relative. And while the mind is no longer in that state of being solely one with the Absolute, it does have a remembrance of the experience. It is like the taste of the banana. We only have the actual taste of a banana when it is on our tongue and we are eating it. Does that mean that after we are done eating a banana, we no longer know the taste of the banana? Not at all. We know the taste, but we know it as a remembrance.

What enables us to have an ego, a sense of self? Our brain and central nervous system. Our brain and central nervous system provide the platform to host our mind. As long as we have a living, breathing body with a functioning mind, we will have a sense of self. But there is a world of difference between the sense of self of a pre-self-realized mind and a post-self-realized one. Let's try to go through how this all takes place, looking at the brain/mind complex as if it were a computer.

When we are first born, we have a brain and mind that function, but have not yet been programed (except for automatic functions that are beyond our control: Breathing, digestion, circulation, etc.). What programs our active brain/mind? Well, it kind of self-programs using a database that is inputted to it by the senses. Our senses load all this information into our brain, which flows over to the mind, thus giving it what it needs to develop. At first our brain/mind really does not know much of anything. It doesn't know that this newborn baby, this body, is a separate being from its mother. It doesn't understand space and distance. It can't work its limbs, has no coordination, and no control over its bodily functions of elimination. It can't name or label anything because no language has been downloaded. Immediately the senses start sending information to the brain in the form of electrical impulses, which the brain then decodes. The brain categorizes all the information it receives from the senses, and formulates knowledge based upon that information. But the information sent to the brain is severely limited, as the senses perceive only the relative, and only that part of the relative that falls within their narrow purviews of perception. As such, all knowledge gained, either directly or by inference from this restricted gathering of information, is subject to the same limitations. These limitations also spill over to our sense of self. We believe that we are these individual, limited beings contained within the confines of our physical bodies; beings that came into existence with this event called birth, and exit on this event called death.

So what happens to our mind and sense of self as we move along on our spiritual journey? Typically, the first event to getting onto a path of self- discovery is that we read or hear something about higher states of consciousness, self-realization, this thing called "enlightenment." We may read something that tells us that this world around us is not real and that what is real is this hidden, mystical, all-pervading consciousness. Further research suggests that this new way of viewing things may be somewhat akin to what the various religions are saying, although religions are using words like "God" and "Soul." None of this makes much sense, as it all seems to be going against the information that our five senses have been providing to our brains; information that has been used in programing our minds. In any event, this new information is taken in, and our minds start to reprogram, using this new data that suggests that maybe there is a reality that is different from that provided by our senses, although exactly what this new reality is, is totally unknown. We decide to take the next step and we learn to meditate to see if we can gain some type of experience to go along with this new intellectual information that we have been gathering.

So now, instead of the mind turning outward, as it habitually does as it gathers data from the senses, our meditation turns the mind inward toward its source, the seat from which the mind's thoughts originate. As the mind settles, thoughts become subtler and subtler and eventually drop away altogether as we pass into a new state of consciousness, the transcendence. We go in and out of this transcendental state as we meditate, gaining a new type of awareness, an awareness that was not made known to us by our sense-programed mind. This new awareness is very charming, and there is the sense that this is actually our real state of being, our true Self. Our mind now starts to update all its original programing, using the knowledge and experience gained from our quest for self-realization. Our contact with the Absolute causes massive amounts of stress to release, and our nervous system begins to rewire itself. Our mind is now functioning under two separate programs; a relative one that has been programed using information gathered from the senses, and another one that is being programed using the knowledge and experience gathered as we turn inward in our search for self-realization. Things around us start to take on a dual reality: A relative reality and an Absolute reality. Our sense of self is no longer limited to the confines of our bodies, as we have acquired both knowledge and experience that tells us that this is just not the case.

And then it happens. In an instant, and without warning, the Absolute rips the electrical plug to our mind's computer out of the 110-volt wall outlet that it has been plugged into since birth, and plugs it directly into its nuclear, mega-trillion-volt source. There is an explosion of consciousness and the mind's computer is blown. But due to the restructuring of the mind and central nervous system that has been taking place during our quest for self-realization, there has not been a total meltdown. The old program based on the sense-gathered information is still there; it has just been totally overridden, reprogramed by the Absolute. This is the death of the ego and the emergence of the Self. The mind has merged into its source; the true "Born Again" event has happened. Everything is now experienced as it truly is, with no filtering by the sense-programed mind: No chatter, no labels, no judgment. There is no feeling of liberation, as that is just the companion, the flipside of bondage; there is just Pure Consciousness; a consciousness that doesn't contain the manifest universe—a consciousness that IS the manifest universe. The mind is still there to experience all, but we are no longer the mind, as ignorance has been removed, leaving us with what was always there: The illumination; the light. The mind, having merged into its source, now takes on its true nature: That of illumination. We are not the void, but the illumination; the light that gives us cognizance of the void. There is an awareness that seems to have a substance to it, a thickness, almost like a fog, and everything is enveloped in this awareness. But we are not the awareness, but rather the platform on which awareness rests. We are the subtlest of the subtlest. And while our mind is now established in the Absolute, it continues to have the input of the senses and can still pay attention to the immediate reality of the relative. It still knows to brush the teeth in the morning, and not to step in front of that moving bus!

CHAPTER 34

What's It All About?

Has anyone ever come up to you and asked if you have heard about such and such, and you say, "No, enlighten me?" What did you mean by "enlighten me?" What you wanted was for that person to give you all the information they had on the subject or situation so that you could have a complete understanding of what they were talking about. And why would you want that complete understanding? So that you could know exactly what was going on and respond appropriately. So what is this so called "enlightenment," and why should anyone be interested in seeking it? Enlightenment is gaining a complete understanding of what is really going on WITH EVERYTHING. Not everything in the relative, such as how to fix a car engine or what will be the next winning lottery numbers, but everything in the Absolute; that being: The *underlying* truth of ourselves and everything in the universe that our senses perceive, *and* that which is beyond their range of perception. And why would we want to have this understanding, this awareness of reality? So that we can live life in the way that this creation meant for it to be lived: In its fullest glory and majesty, or, as Jesus preached, to live life in that kingdom of God that lies within.

The nature of life is to evolve, to move forward, and just as the nature of an apple seed is to grow into an apple tree and produce fruit, the seed doesn't need to *do* anything, as it is all in its nature. The nature of mankind is for each individual to reach his or her fullest potential. But everything has its own time. Not everyone is interested in enlightenment; in fact, very few are. That's okay. Only a fortunate few are born with an innate desire to reach out beyond the relative and into the Absolute. Others have no apparent interest, but as soon as they hear of "enlighten-ment," or whatever name one puts on it, something dor-mant inside of them is sparked, and they're onboard and off for the quest. But for the rest, why should they spend time looking for some unknown, hidden thing, when the world is full of wonder and has everything that they seem-ingly need? As one Christian minister stated when asked on TV what he thought about the gospels that were found in the Nag Hammadi Library, "Why would I want to read those? Four is enough for me."

Imagine the world that we experience as just one giant movie. When you go to the movies, you sit back in your seat and you enjoy. With the world, you wake up in the morning and you enjoy. Now let's just say that for every movie you ever went to, you had worn a blindfold and ear-plugs. You couldn't see or hear anything, but the seats were comfortable, and the popcorn was great, and you always enjoyed the "show." Now one day you go to the movies and sit back with your bag of popcorn, but just before the mov-ie starts, someone comes by and removes your blindfold and takes out your earplugs. How's the movie? What words could you possibly use to describe the difference between a movie seen with a blindfold and earplugs on, and one seen with the blindfold and earplugs off? Now you may say: I see your analogy, but I don't have a blindfold and earplugs on when I go out into the world. And this, my friend, is the very heart of the issue. For, more correctly, instead of you saying, "I don't have a blindfold and earplugs on," what you *should* have said was, "I don't *believe* that I have a blindfold and earplugs on." As we stated in the very beginning of this book, our beliefs and opinions are based on things that we consider to be true, and as our understanding of what is true changes, so do our beliefs and opinions. But what are these so-called blindfolds and earplugs that we have on? They are ignorance and forgetfulness. And again, what is it that we are we ignorant and forgetful of? It is that the *creation* is not separate and distinct from the *creator.* Ignorance lies in the belief that the apparently ever-changing relative is separate and distinct from the never-changing Absolute.

Let's just examine one of our senses. Let's take sight. Do you really believe that you have ever seen anything as it truly is? You do? Interesting. Who is seeing and what are they seeing? Let's take a look at how we "see." Light reflected from an object passes through our corneas. This light then passes through a lens, which focuses the light, or image, onto the photoreceptor cells in our retinas. These cells then convert the light into electrical signals, which are further processed and sent to our brains by way of our optic nerve. We actually "see" with our brains. Our brains are seeing, not our eyes. And who is actually "seeing" inside our brain? Is there a little person in there watching a monitor? And what is this little person seeing? Are they actually seeing the object that the eyes are looking at? No! They are just seeing the light that is being reflected from the object.

Take a piece of gold jewelry and set it on a table. Does it move? Is it alive? No? Are you sure? If you were to take a tiny particle of gold from your piece of jewelry and place it under a very powerful electron microscope, you could see the atoms moving around! Are you still sure that that piece of jewelry isn't moving? Are you still sure that it's not alive? Do dead things move around? Just because something can't be seen, doesn't mean that it's not there. And just because you can perceive something, doesn't mean it's real.

So again, how is this world like a great, big, wonderful movie to the enlightened? While they are seeing and hearing all that we see and hear, they realize that it is all a play of consciousness, with all the ups and downs, heroes and villains, there for our entertainment. Just as a movie would be very boring without its scoundrels and desperadoes, tragedies and triumphs, this world has all the makings for a truly entertaining epic. And how do the enlightened go through life always enjoying the "show" without ever getting sucked into all the craziness, all the apparent heartache? While they are seeing and hearing the same performance that we see and hear, with all the constant and unending changes going on, they are also *seeing* and *hearing* what is going on behind the scene, behind the curtain. And just what is going on behind the curtain? That, you will have to discover for yourself.

CHAPTER 35

What's Important?

What's important to you? Is it your family, your health, your job? Maybe it's a pet, a classic car that you have restored, or a piece of jewelry that belonged to your grandmother. Different things are important to different people. Does the importance of things change for us as we move forward on the spiritual path? Yes, it does. The importance of things changes simultaneously in diametrically opposed, polar opposite ways: Everything is of the most importance, while at the same time nothing is of any importance at all! How is this possible? Well, on the outside, the self-realized individual continues to act according to his or her own nature, but on the inside they do not act at all. There is no movement on their part. All movement is that of the unmoving Absolute "moving" through them. They are just the conduit, the empty vessel, through which all appears to be happening: "Not my will, but thine, be done." While everything they do is done with the utmost attention, none of the results are of their doing, as they do not "do" anything. They are inherently aware of the apparently contradictory nature of everything, that being, the underlying, unchanging Absolute nature of the universe, with its constantly changing, relative aspect, superimposed upon it. As such, it may appear to others that they have the seemingly contradictory attitude that everything is important and nothing is important.

So how does this work? Let's say you are washing dishes in your kitchen. As you do, you wash, dry, and put your dishes away as if it was the most important thing in your life, and actually, as you do this activity, it would be the most important thing in your life, and your full attention would be on the task at hand. Someone offers to help, and as they are putting away one of your dishes, a dish that has been in your family for over 100 years, they accidentally drop it and it shatters into a million pieces. Your reaction: No big deal; it was just a dish.

By analogy, this principle of everything is important and nothing is important is incorporated into the study and practice of T'ai Chi Ch'uan under the saying, "Treat the real as unreal and the unreal as real." T'ai Chi translates as "Supreme Ultimate." Ch'uan as "Fist." Thus we have, "Supreme Ultimate Fist" (or "Fighting"). At its highest level, T'ai Chi Ch'uan is the ultimate martial art for self-defense. It is based on principles of balance, relaxation, and acute sensitivity, whereby one relaxes the body and refuses to exert any force or tense one's muscles against an opponent's assault, thus "giving up oneself and yielding before the opponent." The practice of T'ai Chi Ch'uan has two aspects: The Solo Exercise, where one practices the postures of the form on their own; and Pushing-Hands Practice, where two players stand facing each other with their feet in fixed spots as they try to "uproot" their opponent by causing both of their opponent's feet to leave the ground at the same time, while they themself remain fully rooted to the ground, in a balanced, relaxed stance.

In push-hands practice, your instinctive reaction is to stiffen up and resist your opponent's push on you. This is where you must totally "let go" and treat the real as unreal. In solo practice of the form, it is much easier to stay relaxed, as here we have no opponent pushing on us. This is where we must imagine an opponent and treat the unreal as real. These principles of yielding, effortlessness, and "emptying" all come into play as we journey through life, meeting its "important" challenges with the natural attitude of "treating the real as unreal and the unreal as real."

As we move along on the spiritual path, there is no need to *try* to act in a certain way. To do so only creates an artificial mood. We just act according to our own nature, a nature that continues to evolve spontaneously to be more in accord with the natural law of the Absolute; that being one based on peace and tranquility. We just do our sadhana (spiritual practices), and all changes happen automatically from the inside out. This is not to say that we never try to act in a certain way when our initial impulse may be to act in a way that we believe to be inappropriate. This is the "fake it till you make it" principle. Let's say that every morning I want to give my neighbor's dog a little kick as I walk by him on my way to work. I know that this is an inappropriate thing to do, but still, this is my impulse. What to do? Fake it till I make it. I continue to resist the urge to give that little kick to my neighbor's dog until the impulse is no longer there. Once this urge is gone, I can act toward my neighbor's dog in accordance with my now more evolved nature, that being to give him a little pat on the head as I walk by!

Many believe that if you strive to exhibit the virtuous character traits of someone like Jesus, that you too will attain their level of consciousness, their level of Godliness. This is putting the cart before the horse. The traits that Jesus displayed: Compassion, kindness, charity, etc., were a *result* of his level of consciousness, not the *cause* of it. While one can never go wrong in trying to live a virtuous life, if it is only coming from your head, and not from your heart, it may just be a fictitious display of righteousness and not a natural outpouring of your true nature. Do your sadhana, keep your focus on realizing the Ultimate Truth, and there will be no need to be concerned with your actions, as all your actions will be a reflection of your true nature. And what is your true nature? That you must realize for yourself.

Once there was a king who wanted to see how an enlightened person acted, so he invited a self-realized saint to spend the day with him. The king and the saint rose together, brushed their teeth, had some tea, went for a long walk in the king's gardens, and then went back to the king's chambers for lunch. As they ate, the king said to the saint that he did not see any difference in their actions and that the saint appeared to be living his life no differently from how the king lived his. The saint said, "Oh no, your majesty, we live our lives in a totally different manner."

The perplexed king asked, "How so?"

The saint explained, "First off, as you were brushing your teeth this morning, you were thinking about all the things you had to do today, all your duties. As I was brushing my teeth, the only thing I was doing was brushing my teeth. As you were having your tea, you were thinking about the food stocks for the coming season, and comparing your tea to last year's harvest and wondering how next year's tea would turn out. I, on the other hand, was solely drinking my tea. As we walked through the gardens, your mind was racing with concerns about a multitude of unrelated things. I, again, was only in the garden enjoying my walk. For you see, your highness, I live my life in the moment; you live your life everywhere but in the moment."

As you embark on your spiritual journey, it is important to lead a simple life. But please understand: You can have all the luxuries of the world and still lead a simple life.

CHAPTER 36

In Summary

Sat-Chit-Ananda is a compound Sanskrit word comprised of Sat (existence), Chit (consciousness), and Ananda (bliss), three terms that are considered inseparable from the Absolute, the Ultimate Reality. They represent, if you will, three attributes of the attributeless Ultimate Truth, a Truth which is none other than our very Self.

No one doubts his or her own existence, and, as such, we do not try to discover if we exist. We may, however, misguidedly attempt to discover our Self. Misguidedly, for if we are looking for it one second into the future, we have jumped past it; if we are looking for it one inch in front of us (as something different), we have skipped over it, for that which we seek is right here and now. We don't experience existence, we *are* existence, and that existence IS Self!

Why is it that we have an innate desire to be happy? It is because happiness is our very nature, the nature of the Self. Not knowing this, we use our senses to search for happiness on the *outside*. We think people, places, and things make us happy, so we attempt to gather as much of this outside stimuli as we can in order to obtain happiness. But what we perceived on the outside is not the Ultimate Truth; it is the relative, which is impermanent and subject to change. Someone or something may make us happy, but only fleetingly. When the Self is realized, we have permanent happiness, which is so great, so all-encompassing, that it has been referred to as Bliss, the very nature of the Ultimate Truth, our Self.

The mystic, philosopher, and scientist all seek the same thing: The Ultimate Truth of the universe and all that it contains. But our common search is not one for volumes of individual bits of information to all be put together like pieces of some gigantic jigsaw puzzle. What we seek is very simple. In fact, it is the simplest of the simplest. What we seek is the oneness of it all, what Einstein termed: the Unified Field Theory, or Theory of Everything, a simple means of understanding and tying together all phenomena in existence.

While on the surface this universe appears to be filled with infinite diversity, underneath it all lies the unity of the Ultimate Truth, a truth that is of the nature of consciousness, and has been referred to as everything from God, Allah, or Brahman, to the Absolute, Pure Consciousness, or Self. We cannot speak the Ultimate Truth; we can only talk *about* it, surround it with words, words that, no matter how lofty, only create mental concepts that are anything but the Ultimate Truth. You, along with everything else, are what you were before there was anything, before this universe came to be, and, as such, you need not do anything to be what you already are. But if we already are this Pure Consciousness, this Ultimate Truth, why don't we know it? How could we ever become ignorant or forgetful of our own true nature?

Why do we get chills up and down our spine when we go to a horror movie, or cry when we watch a tearjerker? After all, they're just movies. Even though we know we are watching a movie, we get pulled in and become one with the whole movie experience, become a part of what's going on. Ever walk into a room in the middle of a really tense scene of a scary movie? Everyone in the room is watching this fright-flick on TV, their fingernails digging into the arms of their chairs, and we walk in and start watching, and we're not scared at all. In fact, we may even find it a little comical that everyone else is so scared. What's going on? Well we just started watching, so we are fully aware that it's only a movie, while everyone else in the room has been completely drawn in, become "attached"; they have come to be a part of the movie. And movies do this using only two of our senses: Sight and sound. The "real" world does it using all five of our senses.

Our belief in what is real or unreal is based upon information provided to us by our senses, and our senses provide just the right amount of information for us to function in this seemingly real world. What if you could smell as well as a dog, whose sense of smell is 10,000 to 100,000 times more acute than ours? Do you really want to be eating dinner in your house and smell every dog that walks by outside, even when all your windows are closed? How about having an intimate dinner with your significant other at your favorite restaurant. Would you really want to hear as well as the greater wax moth, a creature that hears 150 times more than humans do? Not only would you be hearing the conversations of everyone else in the restaurant, they would all be hearing every word of your conversation, just as if they were sitting right at your table with you during your "intimate" dinner. And how about walking across that 100-foot ballroom floor—why don't you lose your balance and fall over as you walk across the room? Why would you, you ask? Well those molecules of that solid wood floor are about 99.9999% empty space, meaning that the "solid" area of that 100-foot floor you just walked across is about as wide as the thickness of a human hair. Maybe it is better that our eyes and the rest of our senses don't perceive things as they truly are.

Now it's not that we are trying to say that a tree, or pen, or coffee cup is not real, after all, everyone sees these things; how could they not be real? Our concern is not whether or not they are real; our interest is in the *nature* of their reality. But please understand—not everything is meant to be understood. To the enlightened, the words *real* or *unreal* have no meaning; there just "is." There is a story about an enlightened sage who was talking to some townspeople about the nature of reality, explaining that all that we perceive is just Maya (illusion). Later that day, a couple of boys witnessed a tiger chase the sage, who then ran and climbed up a tree to get away. From a safe distance, the boys yelled to the sage, asking if everything was just an illusion, why did he run and climb the tree when the tiger chased him. The sage's answer, "It is all just an illusion; all you saw was an imaginary tiger chasing my imaginary body up this imaginary tree!"

We are attempting to understand the Ultimate Reality, a reality that comprises everything, including ourselves. But due to the structure of the mind, we can only know something else; we can't know ourselves, as the very nature of knowing requires the triad of a knower, something to be known, and the act of knowing. But the Ultimate Reality does not have a knower and something else to be known. It just sits alone, so to speak, a silent knowing with nothing to know. So as there is no "you" to know or understand something "else"; all you need to do is drop the false notion that you are somehow separate.

Reality can be viewed as having two aspects: The relative and the Absolute, which together form the whole. One aspect is always changing, while the other remains ever the same. And while the seemingly apparent, relative aspect is discernible to the senses, and there for all to grasp and understand, the Ultimate Truth, the Ultimate Reality, though part and parcel of the relative, is not an object to be perceived. It is not a thing to become cognizant of and then comprehended. It is not something to be illuminated. It *is* the illumination. The illumination that lets us see what's there and experience what is not; the light that illuminates all, including itself. You are always aware. Just be the awareness!

If you were to remove this false ignorance and remember your true, enlightened nature, what words could you use to describe this true Self to others? Jesus chose the words, "I and my Father are one." What words would "God" use? When God appeared to Moses from within the burning bush, Moses asked who should he say God was. The response: "I am who I am." God later referred to himself as "I am." For anyone merged with the Absolute and trying to answer the question of who they were, the only answer could be: "I am." Not: I am "this" or I am "that," for any word coming after "I am," even the word "God," would put a limit, a boundary, on the pure "I am." Even saying: "I am limitless" puts a boundary on I am, as anything that is limitless can't be limited. If Sri Ramana Maharshi were to be asked to describe his true nature, his response would either be one of two. He would either answer his questioner with silence, or he would advise them to seek their own true nature; to answer for themselves the question of: "Who am I?" and then see if they still had the desire to ask their question of him.

Our search is one of self-realization, the answer to the age-old question of "Who am I?" We, and everything else in the universe, are only that which existed before there was anything; something we have been referring to as the "Ultimate Truth," an immutable truth that is beyond both time and space. It is a truth that cannot be heard with ears; you will not hear it spoken in a church, mosque, synagogue, temple, or cave. It is a truth that cannot be seen with eyes; you will not see it written in the Bible, Koran, Torah, Bhagavad Gita, or I Ching. This Truth that we seek is not one that you can touch with your finger or pick up with your hand. It is *no* where, yet *every* where. It is *no* thing, yet *every* thing. Knowing this Truth to be none other than his own Self, Jesus proclaimed to the world that he was "The Truth." And how about you? What will this Truth do for you when you realize that it is none other than your own Self? —The Truth shall set you free!

******

If you didn't already have an interest in looking for that buried treasure that's hidden inside the hearts of all humankind, I hope that this book may have sparked some, and that you are now ready to pick up that shovel and start digging. For those of you who are already on the path, I wish you well.

As I stated in my introduction, our medium of communication has been language—words—the medium of the mind and intellect, and, as such, all that I have been able to espouse in this book have been concepts, ideas, and thoughts, and no matter how close we get, we always miss our mark. I have not really been able to share any of the "beingness" that I wanted to share in this book, knowing even before I put my first words to paper that it would be an impossibility, as these things can't even be thought of, much less articulated. Even ultimate experiences or re-alizations can't be experienced or realized, as that would require the triad of the knower, the known, and the act of knowing. There is nothing to know and no one to know it. There just is! Recognizing these limitations, I would still like to leave you with one last question to ponder: "Is God in that bottle cap?"

NOT A RESEARCH PROJECT

This has not been a research project. These are my experiences and my understandings, coming from years of meditating, doing T'ai Chi and qigong, reading hundreds of books on a multitude of topics (including religion, martial arts, and spirituality), and spending countless hours in self-reflection. The concepts in this book are not of my creation; all have been espoused by others before me. I am not "enlightened" or even close to it. Nor will I ever become enlightened for (and please don't tell my wife and kids) there is no me. I'm just this seemingly nutty, crazy guy, who has learned not to take anything too seriously, as all is not as it appears!

Suggested Readings

This is a very short list to start you on your way. I find that the more you read, from a wide variety of perspectives, the more things start to make sense. All books, including these, can only provide a basis for intellectual knowledge and understanding. It is imperative that you include a daily meditation practice in order to have the experience needed to make sense of what you read. I also find it very helpful to go back and reread books after a few years of meditating, as your understanding of what you read will grow exponentially with your experience of meditation.

One thing to keep in mind: Words may be true or untrue, depending upon the level of understanding, but to the enlightened the words *true* or *untrue* have no meaning.

Suggested readings (in no specific order):

An Introduction to Zen Buddhism by D. T. Suzuki

The Secret Path by Paul Brunton

The Untethered Soul: the journey beyond yourself by Michael A. Singer

The Gnostic Gospels by Elaine Pagels

Talks with Sri Ramana Maharshi by Sri Munagala Venkataramiah

The Science of Being and Art of Living by Maharishi Mahesh Yogi

God Loves Fun by Sri Sri Ravi Shankar

I Am That: Talks with Sri Nisargadatta Maharaj by Nisargadatta Maharaj

Autobiography of a Yogi by Paramahansa Yogananda

The Cloud of Unknowing & the Book of Privy Counseling edited by William Johnston, foreword by Huston Smith

The Universe and Dr. Einstein by Lincoln Barnett

Maharishi Mahesh Yogi On The Bhagavad-Gita: A New Translation and Commentary Chapters 1–6 by Maharishi Mahesh Yogi

A Search in Secret India by Paul Brunton

Vasistha's Yoga by Swami Venkatesananda

ABOUT THE AUTHOR

John D. Sambalino received his Juris Doctor and Master of Laws in Taxation from the University of Florida. Since early childhood, he has had the sense that the world that surrounds us is not as real as it appears and that there must be some unknown, hidden truth underlying all that we perceive. He has dedicated his life to uncovering this hidden reality, and in addition to having read over 300 books on spirituality, religion, and martial arts, he has meditated two to three hours a day, ***every day***, for over forty years, practiced yoga and tai chi for over forty years, and qigong for over twenty years. Sambalino is a venture capitalist involved in real estate, solar energy, and 3D technology. He has executive produced three movies, including *The Four-Faced Liar* which won the 2010 HBO Audience Award For Best First Feature Film. Sambalino is an avid stand up paddleboard surfer, and he lives with his wife, Niki, in southern New Jersey.